CONTENTMENT

Also by Robert A. Johnson

He: Understanding Masculine Psychology

She: Understanding Feminine Psychology

We: Understanding the Psychology of
Romantic Love

Inner Work:
Using Dreams and Active Imagination for
Personal Growth

Ecstasy: Understanding the Psychology of Joy

Femininity Lost and Regained

Transformation:
Understanding the Three Levels of
Masculine Consciousness

Owning Your Own Shadow:
Understanding the Dark Side of the Psyche

The Fisher King and the Handless Maiden:
Understanding the Wounded Feeling Function in Masculine and
Feminine Psychology

Lying with the Heavenly Woman:
Understanding and Integrating the
Feminine Archetypes in Men's Lives

Also by Robert A. Johnson and Jerry M. Ruhl

Balancing Heaven and Earth: A Memoir

CONTENTMENT

A WAY
TO TRUE
HAPPINESS

ROBERT A. JOHNSON
AND
JERRY M. RUHL

HarperSanFrancisco
A Division of HarperCollins*Publishers*

HarperCollins books may be purchased for educational, business, or sales promotional use. For information please write: Special Markets Department, HarperCollins Publishers, 10 East 53rd Street, New York, NY 10022.

HarperCollins Web Site: http://www.harpercollins.com

HarperCollins®, ♨®, and HarperSanFrancisco™ are trademarks of HarperCollins Publishers Inc.

FIRST EDITION
Designed by Joseph Rutt

Library of Congress Cataloging-in-Publication Data
Johnson, Robert A.
Contentment : a way to true happiness / Robert A. Johnson and Jerry M. Ruhl. — 1st ed.
p. cm.
ISBN 0-06-251592-6 (Cloth).
ISBN 0-06-251593-4 (pbk.)
1. Contentment. I. Ruhl, Jerry M. II. Title.
BJ1533.C7J64 1999
152.4'2—dc21 98-49365

99 00 01 02 03 ❖/RRD (H) 10 9 8 7 6 5 4 3 2 1

CONTENTS

❧❧

Contents

Contents

Contents

PREFACE

This book has been incubating for several years. It began with a lecture by my friend and colleague, Robert A. Johnson, who applied the powerful and profound story of King Lear to examine some ways that modern people sabotage their own contentment. We tend to look for something or someone on the outside to make us feel satisfied and complete, but contentment isn't found out there. It is an inner experience. The word itself, *contentment,* carries the implication of *content*—to be at home with what you already contain. Realizing this can save you a lot of misdirected energy and put you on a more fruitful path.

During the past year Robert and I worked together, drawing upon depth psychology and many spiritual traditions as well as the genius of Shakespeare, to develop a more complete understanding of contentment. You don't need to be a sage sitting on a mountaintop to be content, but these days it does require some uncommon thinking.

As modern people, we like to believe that contentment comes from getting what we want. It does not. Contentment grows out of our capacity to mediate our desires with "what is." A basic spiritual principle is learning to accept "what is" instead of insisting that life be a certain way. Life is rarely the way we want it to be; it's just the way it is. This doesn't mean that you should give up or become passive. The art of realizing contentment is an active and dynamic process. You might imagine it as a dance between your wishes and reality, what you want and what you get. This doesn't have to be a struggle. Perhaps you've seen old movies featuring the great dance team of Fred Astaire and Ginger Rogers. Fred and Ginger developed a wonderful shared rhythm, two entities so responsive to each other that there was no longer a sense that one was leading and the other following. As one stepped forward, the other stepped back. They moved as one. This is how each of us can learn to dance with what is given. Sometimes you take the lead and assert your will, and fate moves with you. In the very next step you may need to follow rather than lead. Clearly, to move with such agility and grace takes a lot of practice, but our practice studio is daily life.

We live in a transitional, complicated age, perhaps the adolescence of humankind, so contentment requires effort on our part. The goal of this book is to provide readers with both practical strategies for the mind and rich nourishment for the soul.

I would like to thank Robert for his faith in this project and the guidance he has provided throughout its development. I also owe a debt of gratitude to the faculty at Pacifica Graduate Institute, in particular Dr. Charles Asher, Dr.

Robert Romanyshyn, Dr. Dianne Skafte, and Dr. Mary Watkins, who shared many rich ideas in lectures and conversations. Finally, I wish to thank my wife, Jordis, and son, Oliver, for providing the most meaningful content in my life.

Jerry M. Ruhl, Ph.D.

September 25, 1998

Denver, Colorado

PART I

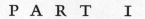

THE
TRAGEDY
OF
MODERN
DISCONTENT

CHAPTER I

"JUST AS SOON AS . . ."

Who does not want contentment? Yet in our modern lives there is an epidemic of discontent. It is the tragedy of our times that no matter what we achieve, how much money we earn, or how many blessings come our way, more is never enough. For every desire you fill, another one always follows just on its heels. You may own a house in Aspen and make more money than God or Bill Gates, but still the feeling of fullness keeps slipping away. That's because contentment is not the result of what you have or even what you do in life. Contentment isn't out there. Well, maybe there are small tastes of it out there, but those tastes stop satisfying after a short time and then you hunger for more. And try as you might, no amount of possessions, power, or prestige satisfies for long.

Consider a time when you were really content. Nearly everyone can think of moments when their inner yearning was filled. Maybe you were watching your child eat his first birthday cake or take her first steps. What a satisfying, fulfilling experience! Perhaps you were out fishing on a tranquil mountain lake or walking peacefully in the woods, far away from the deadlines and pressures of work and the insistent nagging of chores around the house. Contentment can also occur in work—those times when you seem to fall into rhythm with your tasks. Instead of glancing up at the clock every few minutes, you engage fully with what you are doing, and time slips by. Attainment of a goal may bring contentment for a while.

But such moments fade all too quickly. Often you don't know that you have walked across a corner of heaven until days or weeks later, when you become nostalgic for what is missing. Then you try to reproduce the conditions that led to your contentment. You bake another cake or return to the woods. But it's never quite the same.

Contentment is hard to maintain. These days, how does one realize inner stillness, satisfaction, and peace of mind?

Our society teaches us that the only reality is the one we can hold onto. It values outer experiences and material possessions. Accordingly, we look for contentment "out there" and live with a "just as soon as" mentality. "Just as soon as I get my work done, I can relax." "Just as soon as I get married, I will be content" or, conversely, "Just as soon as my divorce comes through, I will be content." "Just as soon as I earn enough money I can spend time with my kids." "Just as soon as I get a nicer boss, a better job, a bigger house, a new car. . . ." And so our contentment slips through our fingers like quicksilver—another time, a different place, a better circumstance.

"Just As Soon As" should be printed on dollar bills, replacing "In God We Trust" as the great American slogan. What a painful way to live!

Powerful Purveyors of Discontent

Madison Avenue understands our hunger for contentment and uses it as the basis for modern advertising. Soup, automobiles, life insurance—any and all things are sold with a promise either of the satisfaction they will bring or the discomfort they will help us avoid. Advertising infiltrates nearly every corner of modern life, from television and radio commercials to newspapers, magazines, bumper stickers, billboards, park benches, T-shirts, the Internet—even our home telephones. All these messages are designed to manipulate us into craving some product or service. We are pulled by desires and pushed by fears. Madison Avenue and the mass media are powerful purveyors of discontent.

The great twentieth-century novelist James Joyce, in reflecting on the role of art in society, pointed out that propaganda is designed to create feelings of desire or loathing in the mind of an audience. Desire urges us to possess, to go to something, while loathing urges us to abandon, to go away from something. Joyce contrasted this with art, which he said should elevate the human mind, create an inner stillness, and connect us to what is "grave and constant" in the lot of humankind.

In this way of looking at civilization, much of popular culture today, not just advertising, is simply propaganda aimed at stirring up our discontent. How do you avoid the constant hammering of propaganda in modern life? A good first step is to recognize that chasing after new or different things is never going to satisfy, and your contentment is too important to be lost in an endless cycle of getting and spending, desire and regret.

As you probably already have discovered, doing more of what you have already done up to now is not the answer. More consumer goods, more work, more vacations, more lovers will not lead to more contentment. Instead, you need to develop greater self-awareness and personal understanding. Contentment comes from the inside.

Part 1 of this book explores the meaning of contentment and what its loss has meant for us. Part 2 presents a timeless story to help us understand psychological problems of our age and to suggest some remedies, while parts 3 and 4 present practical techniques and tools for realizing contentment in daily life. It's never too late to drop "just as soon as" and instead begin to realize a more contented life.

CHAPTER 2

IN SEARCH OF CONTENTMENT

What is contentment?

The dictionary informs us that it is the experience of being satisfied, of not desiring more than you have. This is a starting point, but it leaves out important elements of contentment, including the most essential aspects from a psychological perspective. What does it feel like to be contented? What are the conditions that produce contentment?

Recall again a satisfying time when everything seemed right: there was no need to alter what you were doing, who you were with, or where you were. During such moments life is rich and full. The mingled buzz of worries, fears, and anxieties that so often circle your head like a swarm of hungry mosquitoes is quieted. Instead of judging or second-guessing yourself, you are satisfied just to be. Even that old familiar voice of desire, the disturbance in your mind that cries like a needy and demanding child, *I want, I want, I want,* is somehow stilled. Contentment feels peaceful as the moonlight at the bottom of a stream, tranquil amid constant change.

Now. Here. This is it. Contentment gives you a different experience of time; your mind stops wandering into the
past or the future. As modern people, we waste so much
time wishing we were in a different circumstance, which of
course is quite impossible. You could call contentment
being in love with the moment, not just dutifully accepting
it like an arranged marriage but passionately, rapturously
embracing the eternal now as your soul mate.

Contentment grows out of a willingness to surrender
preconceived ideas and affirm reality as it is. Honoring
"what is" is just the opposite of living out of a "just as soon
as" mentality. Reality doesn't always go the way you would
like. When this happens, you can either become frustrated
and redouble your efforts to push reality around, or you can
learn to accept, affirm, and even dance with what is given.
This book is about the dance between what we want and
what reality presents to us. It's all in the dance.

Arusakumar, the Coconut Seller

Mark Twain once said that nothing so broadens a person's
perspective as traveling to a foreign land. It is difficult to see
the assumptions and habits by which you live until you step
out of them.

There is a coconut seller named Arusakumar who lives
in a bamboo shack near the town of Pondicherry in southern
India. He is a master at the art of slicing off the top of a green
coconut with a machete, inserting a straw, and offering it to

customers. You sit on a burlap sack of coconuts to enjoy your drink, as this is the only furniture at his curbside stand. Arusakumar must be one of the most contented men in the world, and this near-divine quality is highly contagious. He sings and laughs and pulls you into a Garden of Eden atmosphere in which he spends each day.

Contentment is beyond the vagaries of fortune or possession. Arusakumar's options are limited, his expectations low, and his contentment high. He still blunders about and gets into difficulties, but when he does, he doesn't feel guilty or obsess about what he could have or should have done.

Arusakumar possesses a profound awareness of an invisible, eternal reality. When things don't go the way he might wish, he assumes that a larger plan is at work. This unseen pattern—call it fate or the will of God—may not be immediately clear, but he trusts that it will eventually be revealed, and he accepts it. How different this is from the modern approach of grabbing life by the collar and throttling it into submission!

Cut Off from Our Roots

It was part of the genius of the Swiss psychiatrist Dr. Carl Jung to recognize that in modern life, the personal self is assigned too great a task. We are taught in Western culture that each of us is a separate, isolated self. We forget that there is a deeper layer of experience that we share with our whole culture and with all creation. This Jung called the collective unconscious—a source of wisdom, purpose, and meaning.

The collective unconscious is a great sea from which we have all been born. In this sea live the feelings, ideas, abilities, behaviors, faults, and virtues that we identify as ourselves; and out of this sea each individual, each ego, each "I," develops.

Many intelligent people today refuse to admit that they have an unconscious. They insist they know why they want what they want, and why they do what they do.

Unconscious is a curious term, like *uncola*. It says what it is not rather than what it is. But the unconscious is not so vague and esoteric. It consists of all those processes taking place in and around you that occur in the background. You know that your blood pressure and rate of breathing adjust when you run up a hill or as the weather changes, and you don't have to consciously think about it. Just as your body does many things without requiring conscious thought, so does your mind. To say that we have an unconscious is another way of saying that we are mentally and physically part of nature. The depths of the unconscious are the depths of nature. Even when we feel most isolated from others, it is important to remember that our common psychological home remains the same.

Dr. Jung raised important questions for modern people concerning the nature of our real self, reminding us of something that earlier civilizations took for granted—that the self lies much deeper than reason and intellect, deeper than our individuality. The exploits of the gods and demons of the ancients may seem fantastic and irrational by today's standards, but at least premodern people were aware of the important fact that there are powerful forces at work in our lives that have an existence of their own independent of our conscious will and desires. To find contentment, we can't just ignore the powers of the unconscious. We must relate to them.

Reconnecting to a Larger Whole

We live in an age of "I" consciousness. Humans dominate the physical world in a way no one thought possible. Our buildings and our cities are monuments to ourselves. Just look at the skyline of a major metropolis; the grandest buildings are symbols of human power, status, and control. Earlier in Western history, the tallest building was always dedicated to the divine. But as we've become skilled at controlling external reality, we also become filled with "God-almightiness."

Not too many years ago the Shell Oil building in London was assembled floor by floor until its height exceeded that of the dome of St. Paul's Cathedral. There was an outcry in the newspapers and tremendous discussion that an old age had passed and a new secular age of commerce and business was replacing traditional values.

Ecological crises of various kinds are teaching us the folly of thinking we can manipulate nature at our whim without serious consequences. All of life is interconnected and interdependent. This applies equally to our inner world.

We get into all kinds of trouble by thinking that life can be measured, understood, and controlled solely through our conscious will. The isolated individual tries to find contentment in novelty, excitement, power, prestige—by manipulating the external world. Cut off from the collective unconscious, we become filled with anxiety and insecurity.

The "I" inside us can become arrogant and alienated from its roots in nature. It is hard for us to admit that there is a great deal in life that is outside our control. But a little humility can be a wonderful gift. Britain's great leader, Winston Churchill, once said, "I have had to eat many of my own words, and I found the diet very nourishing."

Coming Back Down to Earth

We are familiar with the word *humus*, which means rich soil that you add to your garden to make it grow. This is related to the words *humble, humiliate,* and *humility*—all of which involve bringing ourselves back to the earth. Contentment does not require more reasoning and willpower; if that were all that was needed, humanity would surely be content by now. No, instead we must learn to humble our pride and admit that the "I" inside does not know everything and sometimes has a hard time figuring out what is best for us.

Contentment requires that we "soil" the arrogance of modern consciousness by bringing it back down to earth and reestablishing an ongoing relationship with the collective unconscious.

Most psychology today—90 percent or more—ministers to a person's relationship to the outer world. Perhaps you can't get a date or your marriage isn't working or you are socially clumsy or some such thing. These are important issues, and they often require repair work. However, to find contentment, we must attend to the equally wonderful and challenging world within.

There is a story of a spiritual seeker who one day came to his master and asked, "In the olden days it is said that there were people who walked and talked with God. Why doesn't this happen anymore?" The master replied, "Because nowadays no one will stoop so low."

CHAPTER 3

THE FALL FROM EDEN

Infants come into this world whole, in the hands of God. But it doesn't take long for life to become fragmented and complex. Western society encourages us to become as separate, unique, and specialized as possible. We call this "becoming an individual."

We spend our lives working hard to achieve a strong personal self, that sense of "I" that is the center for our doing and having. That "I" demands that we make choices. What is right and what is wrong? Should I choose this or that? This differentiation is necessary, but our civilization pushes the complexity of life to great extremes.

You can make a forceful argument that children should not be subjected to the formal education process too soon or they will be robbed of their childhood. We truncate the childhood of our young ones when we overload them with the too-muchness of modern life. Often there is too little time for fantasy and imagination—the lifeblood of early development.

We might well ask: Is our culture's great emphasis on

individuality really progress? Does it lead to more contented lives or just more production and material goods?

Looking Back for Utopia

Do you have a nostalgic longing for a simpler time? That yearning can be called "utopian thinking." The word *utopia* means a place or situation of moral and social contentment, an ideal condition.

Sir Thomas More stirred the ideals of English citizens when he wrote in 1516 of an imaginary island where people lived in simple contentment. Two centuries later the French philosopher Jean-Jacques Rousseau called for a return to the "noble savage," declaring that civilization was destroying humankind's natural capacity for a rich and happy life.

In nineteenth-century America, Henry David Thoreau left the complexities of his civilization behind to live in a small cabin at Walden Pond. He grew his own food and lived closely and quietly with nature. Thoreau's experiment still touches people and reminds them of their constant hunger for a simpler life.

Eden. Camelot. Atlantis. Shangri-la. We fantasize about magical places where life was pure and simple. We yearn to return to such experience.

Rediscovering Lost Ideals

One of the most thoughtful voices to question the cost of Western civilization was India's great political and spiritual leader, Mohandas Gandhi. Gandhi grew up as a member of the middle class in India, and his early admiration for British civilization was matched only by his outright rejection of India's native culture. In his autobiography Gandhi recounts the shock and embarrassment he experienced during his studies in law school in London when a friend arrived to visit him wearing the Indian *dhoti* or native loin-cloth.

As Gandhi learned firsthand about British culture, however, his praise of Western ways turned to criticism, and he wrote that India was "being ground down under the heel of modern civilization." When Gandhi returned to his native land to lead India's independence movement, he began wearing the simple *dhoti*, and he even spun his own cloth. He was convinced that India should not rush to emulate Western culture.

Gandhi was afraid of losing the virtues of traditional India, and the spinning wheel became his symbol of this. He suggested that everyone in India should spend some time spinning thread to help them remain earthbound. Unfortunately, since his assassination in 1948, Gandhi has been conveniently parked off in the pantheon of saints. Sadly, no Indian today is expected to live up to his ideals of nonviolence, community, and simplicity. Now educated people in India's large cities dance in the streets to celebrate the dangerous proliferation of nuclear weapons.

You don't have to spin thread or weave your own cloth to experience Gandhi's vision of contentment. Utopian thinkers such as he simply call on each of us to rekindle love and honor for the simplest acts of daily life.

You Can Simplify . . .

One path to contentment is to follow the approach advocated by Thoreau and Gandhi: you can simplify. Reducing the sheer number of your daily choices effectively limits what the "I" has to process and cuts out some of the anxiety of modern life.

Do you really need 101 channels on satellite television? Does flipping from channel to channel bring more contentment or less contentment? What are the trade-offs? Apply this yardstick to many things in your life.

We equate freedom with the greatest degree of individuality and the maximum number of choices. Just as an experiment, see what it is like to live with fewer choices. This weekend, rather than going off to consume something, choose to soothe yourself by being quiet, taking a walk in nature, or arranging a simple dinner with friends.

Take an inventory of your life, and look for ways to simplify. Will a new car really bring you more contentment, or will it stretch your budget so you have to work much harder? How long will it be before its "newness" wears off? How about moving to a different house—will the opportunities for enjoyment be offset by worries and innumerable projects? Our doing, just for the sake of doing, is a major factor in modern discontent.

... But Simplicity Isn't Contentment

As part of our hunger for natural contentment, we romanticize pioneers, cowboys, and the "good old days." You can pass a shopping mall or restaurant and see a covered wagon, a plow, or a windmill displayed as decoration. Western movies or stories set amid quaint covered bridges in Iowa or located in the Alaskan wilderness resonate with modern people. This reflects our nostalgia for a golden age.

There is virtue in simplifying your life. It is worthwhile to look for ways to improve your diet, shorten your commute, lower your stress, reduce your debt, and set aside more time for friends and family. However, please be aware that efforts to simplify will ultimately fall short of making you content. Although it may be your fondest wish, there is no going back to the Garden of Eden. Consciousness can only move forward, never backward.

Even with an organic garden and home-baked bread, modern people find themselves beset by discontent. That is because contentment is never the result of doing or having. Rearranging life on the outside cannot produce contentment—at least not for long. Contentment is an inner experience resulting from your level of consciousness.

Climbing Up to Wholeness

The Hindu religion represents the evolution of humankind with a circle. We start at the top in natural contentment, liv-

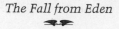

ing instinctively and unselfconsciously. In Jewish and Christian terms, this is the Garden of Eden. Then we fall to the bottom, entering the age of materialism and "I" centeredness. It is from this point we must climb up the other side of the circle to return to whole consciousness.

Our culture specializes in the stage found at the bottom of the circle. It is a partial understanding, a stage of evolution that is no longer rooted in the instinctive world but not yet adequately connected with the heavenly realm.

Remember Arusakumar, the coconut seller who lives in a tiny bamboo shack? Watching this man sing and laugh as he goes about his daily work, you find his natural contentment contagious and you glimpse what is missing in Western society. But this does not mean that to regain contentment we should pack our bags and become street vendors in India. Even if you wanted to leave the Western world behind, trying to take on the simplicity of another culture seldom works (which we can attest to from personal experience).

In traditional societies, such as rural India, the average person does not strive for such intense individuality. There is authority, security, stability, and community. These provide a container that holds and supports people. You are born into a certain profession or caste. You make the most of what you have, and if a troubling question arises you take it to the guru, the holy person, or the head of the village. This was equally true in the West up until about the twelfth century. The priest was the carrier of the splendor of God, and it never occurred to the average peasant that he or she could have our modern sense of individuality. Since then, the West has evolved so that every person wants to be self-directed and given every opportunity, every choice, every freedom.

Living in pre-modern contentment in the West cannot be recovered. We are too much bitten by the bug of individuality. Instead of being caught in the ongoing dilemma of half-consciousness, we must make the journey up the other side of the circle to wholeness.

The Power of Myth and Story

We live in a time when alienation from the unconscious is at its height, but we cannot just throw away our sense of "I." So how do we get outside our current consciousness in order to see beyond it? The human psyche cannot step outside itself to observe from a totally separate vantage point. This is where the power of myth and story can help.

We can use myth and stories to make human experience clear. When a myth moves beyond mere storytelling and truly comes alive for us, we experience deep understanding. Mythic truth helps us find direction and meaning in the midst of life by showing patterns of human experience. Shakespeare's greatest play, *King Lear*, is a rich reference point to help us understand contentment.

It is impossible to say exactly when the modern "I" emerged in Western society. Certainly by Shakespeare's time (1564–1616), having applied reason for many wonder-

ful practical achievements in science and technology, Western people became obsessed with it, so much so that it seemed that we could attain the power of gods. The great bard himself wrote, "What a peece of worke is man, how noble in reason, how infinite in faculties, in form and moving, how expresse and admirable in action, how like an Angell in apprehension, how like a God!"

However, Shakespeare also understood human limitations and frailties. We can read Shakespeare's greatest work, *King Lear*, as a story of the partial consciousness of modern people who, by their own misguided actions, lose their capacity for contentment and experience intense suffering. As the story unfolds, human failings are exposed in full light: ambition, treason, lust, greed, jealousy. Nearly all human relations become distorted. Life becomes a struggle, with the players trying to wrench from life whatever prizes they can grasp. This is a story of modern consciousness. Today, each individual wants to be king of his or her domain, having lost track of the reality that there are many more factors beyond the "I" that must be integrated in ordering a human life and human society.

We want to mine the gold in Shakespeare's great masterpiece, applying its insights to our own time. But before we explore a new psychology of contentment, let's turn to our story and invite the West's most powerful dramatist to speak directly to our hearts.

PART 2

A
STORY
FOR
OUR TIME

CHAPTER 4

KING LEAR

King Lear, Shakespeare's tale of distorted expectations and painful illusions, provides a vivid description of the pervasive discontent accompanying modern life as well as excellent instruction for its cure. It was Shakespeare's inspiration to distill in this story vivid prototypes. Indeed, there is a quality of divine inspiration and profound psychological insight in *King Lear*; it is in many ways a miracle play.

The Lear story is tragic, but it is not without hope or redemption. It shows us characters who are transformed. It must have been rare in Shakespeare's day to find such a person, and it is even more rare today.

As the play opens, the king is about to make a foolish move. Lear has decided to retire and give away his kingdom to his three daughters. He announces that he will apportion the kingdom out by asking the daughters to proclaim how much they love their father. He pries the love out of them. Two of the daughters outdo themselves trying to please the king. Goneril, the oldest, speaks first, saying, "Sir, I love you more than word can wield the matter; / Dearer than eyesight, space, and liberty; / Beyond what can be valued, rich or rare; / No less than life, with grace, health, beauty, honor; / As much as child e'er loved, or father found; / A love that makes breath poor, and speech unable. / Beyond all manner of so much I love you."

The youngest daughter, Cordelia, hears this spectacle of flattery for what it is. "Love, and be silent," she says quietly to herself.

The king's second daughter, Regan, gives another flowery, sentimental speech. Recall Sigmund Freud's definition of sentimentality. He called it "repressed brutality." When sentimentality gushes forth, you don't have to wait very long for brutality to follow, as is painfully borne out in this story.

The two elder daughters give these elaborate, mushy speeches about how much they love their father. Their words are so stilted that they seem to be carefully rehearsed for the occasion rather than spontaneous. They sound immediately insincere, yet Lear is pleased by their polished rhetoric. Then Lear turns to his youngest daughter, Cordelia, and asks, "What about you?"

Cordelia prefers to say nothing, but her father insists that "nothing will come of nothing."

Still, Cordelia demurs. She loves her father deeply, but she understates her affection. This is partly out of honesty and a distaste for hypocrisy, but it also relates to an instinct on her part that something is inherently wrong in what the king is doing.

"I love your Majesty / According to my bond, no more nor less," Cordelia says. By *bond,* Cordelia means the natural obligation between child and parent.

In response to this quiet, honest statement, the king rages, storms about, and ultimately disinherits Cordelia. The angry king declares to his youngest daughter, "Better thou / Hadst not been born than not to have pleased me better."

Many people in our modern world are faced with the awful of dilemma of choosing between unreality or being left alone. If you don't play along with the excesses of our time, you risk being ignored or even tossed aside.

The foolish king, like some would-be god bestowing boons, divides his kingdom up between the two false daughters. The duke of Burgundy, who has been courting Cordelia, leaves her flat when he learns that there will be no inheritance. So much for his love. He reacts like a good materialist, valuing social position, status, power, and possessions. For her honest response, poor Cordelia is abandoned. Luckily, the king of France agrees to take her in.

From this opening scene we already can see that Cordelia is the noblest figure in the story, perhaps one of the noblest characters in all of literature. Her attitude and her words are simple, even plain by modern standards. She offers King Lear the love that is fitting from a daughter—no more and no less.

Legitimate and Illegitimate Creations

Meanwhile, a parallel plot is developing. This story explores the same theme in a somewhat different manner. The earl of Gloucester, also a figure who is high in the court, has two sons, one legitimate and the other illegitimate. Gloucester jokes about the "accidental" birth of his second son, Edmund. He will soon disinherit his legitimate and loyal son, Edgar, as he falls victim to the conniving of his bastard offspring.

Are we so different from Lear and Gloucester? Each of us, in our interior court, produces both legitimate and illegitimate impulses and creations. These may be in our relationships, in our work, or in other parts of our lives. The story suggests that we must consider with care those energies and actions we choose to ally ourselves with and how we divide our resources.

Gloucester's illegitimate son, Edmund, is consumed with ambition. He lives by the law of the jungle, survival of the fittest. He is determined to surpass and destroy his brother, and so he forges a letter suggesting that their father be killed, signs Edgar's name to it, and makes sure that it finds its way to Gloucester.

Just as Edmund schemes against his brother and hungers for his father's wealth and title, Goneril and Regan, Lear's older daughters, also begin to show their true colors once Cordelia is out of the way. In both the story of Lear and the secondary story of Gloucester, we see division and conflict.

As soon as Lear hands over his kingdom, Goneril and Regan become abusive to their father, dismissing his personal guards and thereby stripping the king of his dignity. A loyal supporter named Kent is put into the stocks. This is designed to further undercut and provoke the old king.

Goneril and Regan conspire with Edmund and decide to punish the earl of Gloucester, who has remained loyal to the king. One of the cold-hearted sisters says to hang him, and the other says to pluck out his eyes. We might recall their use of the metaphor of eyesight in an earlier sentimental speech. Goneril had declared her love to be "dearer than eyesight." But now we see where beloved eyesight went: it is to be brutally plucked out.

The metaphor of sight and blindness runs like a continuous thread throughout this story. Those characters who grow and transform begin the play with inner blindness but eventually gain a special kind of vision.

The Dark Night of the Soul

Showered with insults and disrespect, Lear is overcome with rage. He is turned away from the castle, and he sets off into the wild heathlands. It is night, he is wet, and he is miserable. A storm rages through the sky, echoing Lear's own inner turmoil. He appears mad. While shivering out in the rain, Lear speaks to a loyal servant who still attends him. These sublime words may be the most important in Shakespeare's entire play. Lear turns to the servant and asks,

"How dost, my boy? Art cold?" For the first time, the king is paying attention to someone else. He is tending to the servant's coldness in a human way.

This is a turning point in the story; Lear stops ranting about misfortune and how he has been wronged and instead attends to the needs of another person. His redemption begins.

Eventually the king is reunited with Cordelia—the one true daughter, who had been banished from the kingdom. He recognizes how he has wronged her and begs her forgiveness. But soon after reconciling their differences, Lear and Cordelia are taken prisoner by the subversive factions. Surprisingly, this turn of events no longer produces rage in the old king. In fact, Lear seems to accept that life is a prison of sorts.

In the final scene, we learn that Lear has killed the slave who was hanging Cordelia. The old king enters the stage carrying Cordelia's limp body in his arms. Is she dead or alive? Lear brings forth all the tests of the time to see if his beloved daughter might be revived. He places a mirror against her mouth to see if it will fog from a bit of breath. He puts a tiny feather under her nose to see if it might move with the slightest exhalation. Both tests fail.

Transformation of Consciousness

Some literary critics claim that the story of King Lear ends in utter despair and darkness, but the old king who holds

Cordelia in the final scene is not the same man who at the beginning ruled by whim and fancy. He speaks to Cordelia, "You are a spirit, I know. When did you die? Do you see this? Look on her, look her lips, look there, look there!" Then Lear loses consciousness.

Does Cordelia live? Understood as a psychological symbol, yes, she is eternal. Cordelia represents the transformative power of "what is." She is not grasping, manipulative, anxious, inflated, or depressed.

Does Lear live? That is the secret of the play. He certainly gains his enlightenment. Only one character, the loyal Kent, seems to understand the transformation that has occurred. When asked to share in the "rule of the realm," Kent responds mysteriously: "I have a journey, sir, shortly to go. My master calls me; I must not say no."

PART 3

THE PSYCHOLOGY OF CONTENTMENT

CHAPTER 5

CONTENTMENT CAN'T BE FOUND "OUT THERE"—IT'S INSIDE YOU

King Lear introduces us to a timeless kingdom—and for all practical consideration that means your interior life. If you dream of a kingdom or hear the story of a royal court, it should be understood as your interior court. This concerns the drama that goes on inside you. The niceties and stupidities, the failures and the nobility—all of these are aspects of your own life. Keep in mind that the story of King Lear is your story. We will not review every scene or all the subplots and characters in this complex work, for our intent is not to offer literary criticism but rather to understand contentment.

As the play opens, Lear has decided to give the largest share of the kingdom to the daughter who apparently loves him the most. What a horrible thing to do! This is like insisting that your partner declare how much he or she loves you. At that moment, love flies out the window. If you have to pry the love out of someone, authentic feelings run and hide in that very instant. Love must be freely given.

Lear seems to think that love and contentment are commodities that can be bought with his riches. In our materialistic society, we too are led to believe that everything has its price. But love and contentment are not of the material realm. They are invisible spiritual forces.

The king dismisses everyone who wants him to see reality as it is. His lack of self-awareness also means he can't accurately judge the intentions of others. He fails to perceive the insincerity and latent cruelty in his two older daughters as well as in the other schemers surrounding him at court.

Each modern "I" can be likened to a little monarch trying to rule its kingdom. Like Lear, when we mix up the "inner" with the "outer," it is easy to create quite a mess. The first lesson in contentment involves differentiating these two realms—inner and outer. That requires an understanding of projection.

Projection: A Cause for Confusion

Projection is the error of attaching an aspect of your inner life onto someone or something on the outside. This way, you do not have to take responsibility for it. In projecting a disowned part of yourself, you endow other people and things with the power to make you blissful or miserable. Then you turn around and praise or blame the person or situation, while all the while you are reacting to an unconscious, inner part of yourself.

Here are some examples of projection: You are feeling chaotic, so you explode at your co-workers for being disorganized. You dislike your mother's negativity, it drives you crazy, but you fail to see the ways in which you are negative. It is more convenient to project all the negativity onto her. You admire the strength and confidence of the handsome man who lives across the hall and fantasize that if only he would fall in love with you life would be grand—thus you project your inner strength upon a stranger. You dream of living in another town or a different culture where people never catch a cold, neighbors are always generous and kind, and babies don't cry; this is projecting your capacity for contentment onto a different place and circumstance. You don't need to go anywhere to find contentment, but you do need to reel in your projections.

Just like a film projector in a movie theater, your small interior image is projected onto an outer screen. It appears to be an objective fact, and, just as in the movies, it is larger than life, accompanied by strong emotions, dramatic scenes, and twisting plots. Projections change the world into a replica of your own unknown face, involving qualities and emotions that you normally deny in yourself but can plainly see in other people.

Here are two more examples. Suppose your father was a tyrant, and you couldn't wait to grow up and get away from him. You might in later life project the quality of tyranny upon authority figures such as doctors or bosses and have a lot of trouble relating to them. You also are probably driven by an inner tyrant, a hidden part of yourself that is judgmental, demanding, and never satisfied—but you will tend to see and abhor this quality in others rather than in yourself. It is the last thing you want to believe about yourself, so this inner tyrant is projected.

Or suppose you were always daddy's special little girl; as an adult, perhaps you are skilled at getting what you want by being admired and adored. You might easily project your benevolent father on others and expect care and safety without careful discrimination. Your own potential for self-care and self-esteem lies undeveloped in your unconscious, and often you probably find yourself vulnerable to and dependent upon men.

Anytime someone is irritating us out of our wits, we can assume that the cause of our irritation does not lie solely in the other person. At the time it seems abundantly clear that the source of our discontent is "out there"—the store clerk who was rude, the unappreciative co-worker, the negative parent, or the self-centered mate. It's true, the qualities we project can be found "out there"—but they are not a conspiracy to undermine our contentment. Reeling in our projections won't eliminate stupidity and evil in the world, but it can help us sort out inner and outer realities and thereby eliminate a great deal of discontent.

Try this simple exercise. Think of the person you dislike the most. Make a list of the qualities you abhor about them, such as viciousness, backbiting, meanness, being two-faced, cheap, stingy, and so on. Spend a couple of minutes going through your list with a friend or partner. Describe this hated person. Then go through your list a second time and say, "I am . . ." before each quality. Your ego will probably deny it, and you may quickly decide that this is a silly exercise, but if you ponder your list for a while, you might get a glimpse of your own backside.

Everyone projects negative qualities such as laziness, greed, envy, jealousy, scheming, cowardice, fear. We would rather see these qualities in our partners or our neighbors than in ourselves. What is more surprising is that we also project positive qualities. Curiously, people resist the noble aspects of their unconscious even more strenuously than they hide their dark sides.

Reclaiming Your Shadow

Recall that the unconscious is like a great sea from which we have all been born. Jung once defined it as "Everything of which I know, but of which I am not at the moment thinking; everything of which I was once conscious but have now forgotten; everything perceived by my senses, but not noted by my conscious mind; everything which, involuntarily and without paying attention to it, I feel, think, remember, want, and do; all the future things that are taking shape in me and will sometime come to consciousness: all this is the content of the unconscious."[1]

[1]C. G. Jung, *Collected Works* (New York: Bollingen Foundation), 8:185.

The unnoticed, underdeveloped, and unacceptable characteristics in you do not go away; they only collect in the dark corners of your personality like a shadow. They build up energy until they have an opportunity to explode upon the scene. When they have been hidden long enough, they take on a life of their own as projections.

Every person and every civilization has a shadow, and that hidden inner reality is seen through projection. What makes projection so difficult to correct is that it takes place unconsciously. To say that a projection is unconscious means that it *really* is unconscious—that is, outside your conscious control. As a result, you don't make projections so much as meet up with them.

Are Traffic Lights Conspiring Against You?

Here's a useful way to understand projection and its role in undermining contentment. What is the substance of a traffic light? The word *substance* originally meant the spirit behind the material, that which fashions the traffic light, or the spirit of the traffic light. Somehow the meaning of *substance* has taken a 180-degree turn in our modern understanding. People have come to think that substance means the material in the traffic light—some colored glass, metal wire, paint, and plastic. However, the spirit behind the traffic light is a command to stop, slow down, or go. This bit of reality is pretty simple—stop, slow down, or go.

Our projections on the traffic light, however, are much more complicated. You might see that the light is red and think, "Oh, I have to stop again. I'm late. Is fate against me?" Or, you might think, "This damn stoplight is thwarting my progress; why are all these cars in my way?" Many people seem to think, "The light is yellow; this is my chance to speed up and get ahead of everyone." Or maybe, "Yippee, the light's green! I must be living right." All kinds of "I"-centered judgments sneak into this experience, judgments that have nothing to do with the simple reality of stop, slow down, or go. (By the way, as an experiment, for one week the authors carefully observed traffic light encounters and found them to be about equally divided between the colors.)

If you want to see projections in action, just observe yourself in traffic for one day. At each traffic light notice how you attach a projection to the simple reality of stop, slow down, or go.

If a simple traffic light can create so much emotion, what happens in more complex interactions? Consider how much of your day is filled with negative and positive projections distorting your perceptions of the world. When the phone rings or a letter arrives in the mail or you are asked to attend a meeting, do you project qualities—positive or negative—that color your experience? Projections keep us embroiled in illusions of our own making. In Eastern spiritual traditions this is called *maya*, a limited form of consciousness.

When projection is at work, our response is typically: (1) emotional, (2) compulsive, and (3) out of proportion to the reality of the situation. Other people often sense when we are projecting our own hidden qualities upon the world. Unfortunately, we are usually the last to know.

Tending to "What Is"

How can you "reel in" projections and stop blaming the world for your discontent? A good start is to honestly state "what is." Call upon the Cordelia inside you to provide an honest assessment of reality. Sit down and write a "what is" letter. This exercise is not about stating what once was, what might be, or what ought to be. Just state what is. The first attempt at such a letter is almost always too abstract. You will need to be specific. You can't just say, "I'm discontented because my life is a big mess." Try to avoid theory, idealization, and blame. Just state what is. What's the reality of my situation? What's really true of my life here and now? Contentment grows out of the circumstances of life as you find it, in the very place where you currently exist.

When you sincerely state "what is" in any given situation, a mysterious thing happens. "What is" is made conscious, and you are then able to see the next "what is." It becomes clear what you must do next. You do that thing and ask yourself again, "What is?" Then, you do the next right thing. In this stepwise manner you can gradually get your life moving in a positive direction. If you operate out of "what is" instead of living mired in your projections, you can begin to work your way out of any dilemma. When reality is honored, you are speaking from a divine place.

A traffic light is not a conspiracy to frustrate you or steal your contentment, and neither is the reality in which you currently find yourself. It just is. Imagine approaching each circumstance in your day as a simple bit of reality without the projections. Such a day would have a reasonable chance of bringing you more contentment. The more present and aware you are to what is, the greater the possibilities for contentment.

A Special Kind of Projection: Romantic Love

Nearly everyone has had the experience of falling in love—that warm, engaged rapture that lifts you about a foot off the ground. When "in love," you think of the beloved constantly. You can't get enough time together. Even sleep gives no rest. The object of your affection seems heavenly and can do no wrong. This involves a special kind of projection that creates a great deal of disappointment and disillusionment for modern people.

As we all know, the intensity of this "in love" experience changes and ebbs with time. You start to see that "Prince Charming" or "Sleeping Beauty" has some serious flaws. When the intense "in-loveness" starts to change, many people feel somehow betrayed. A James Thurber cartoon captures this moment with genius when a middle-aged man is replying to his wife, "Well, who took the magic out of our marriage?" It is so easy to blame another for the effects of our own projections.

A romantic projection is too much for any human to carry. Whether it lasts for a month, six months, or seven years, eventually it comes crashing down. The wife says, "You are not the white knight like I thought," and the husband says, "You are not the princess I married."

Love cannot be reduced to a psychological mechanism, but it is useful to think of infatuation, that "falling in love" experience, as a force by which we reach out for our own missing qualities. We project our capacity for greater wholeness upon someone else. Recall past loves, asking yourself what you loved about them and what quality they possessed that you wanted to merge with. This will tell you what aspect of your unconscious was yearning to be made conscious.

When a projection no longer holds up against reality, we have a wonderful opportunity to become more whole. For example, it is only after a romantic projection starts to break that a sustainable, human-sized love becomes possible. Human-sized love is based upon knowing a person as she or he really is, not grasping for your own unrealized qualities. Reality is far nobler than any projection.

Differentiating the Inner and Outer Realms

Unfortunately, when reality can no longer sustain our projections, we generally react badly, blaming others for deceiving us or lamenting that the world has not lived up to our expectations. We create embarrassing scenes, slam doors, and shout recriminations. We may withdraw into a shell of our own making—disillusioned and cynical. We would rather cling to a projection than take back our own inner potential. In reclaiming a projection, we are faced with the task of dealing with all the unfairness and devilry that we have attributed to others. If we were to reclaim our projections, then we would no longer have anybody to complain about, nobody to improve or punish, nobody we could blame for our discontent. We also would no longer have anybody to save us, nobody to worship, nobody to look to for our contentment.

In Shakespeare's story, after Cordelia vows to love Lear with the respect due a father, the angry king declares, "Better thou / Hadst not been born than not to have pleased me better." He reacts to Cordelia's simple and honest declaration of "what is" with all the passion of a scorned lover. Please note that there is no queen in Shakespeare's play. A mature partner is missing in this court, and Lear lacks warmth and feeling. Instead of projecting his missing qualities on a queen, Lear places them on his daughters. The king's capacities for relatedness, love, and compassion are all sadly underdeveloped. He wants to command these inner qualities, to acquire them in the outer world like a possession.

When Cordelia refuses to carry the king's projection, he explodes. His response reveals that a projection has been at work: it is emotional, compulsive, and out of proportion to the reality of the situation.

Lear then switches allegiance from Cordelia to his other daughters, which creates even more trouble. Many modern people move from one target for their projection to another, thinking they only have to find the "right one"— the right person, job, situation, or purchase. This is the painful cycle of "contentment will come just as soon as." It takes considerable suffering before Lear is willing to stop blaming others. Unfortunately, it seems that we too will endure all kinds of suffering before we are willing to attend to our inner world.

Projection is a muddling of inner and outer realities. Based on this confusion, we look for contentment "out there." Outer realities have their own intrinsic value. It takes honesty, humility, and courage to reel in our projections, but doing so will bring the objective beauty and value of the outer world into better focus. In differentiating the inner and outer realms, we have a chance to grow psychologically by moving beyond the adolescent quality of viewing the world as a reflection of our own hidden self.

Dangers of Collective Projection

Just as individuals project unconscious parts of who they are, social groups also suffer from this process. Collective projections of negative qualities result in cultural, racial, and religious prejudices and conflicts. All scapegoating is due to projection.

When society worships consciousness and refuses the unconscious, some of the hidden residue appears as hatred, violence, and the other tragedies that fill the morning newspapers. World War II provided many examples of negative projection. One of the most highly civilized nations on earth, Germany, fell into the idiocy of projecting its virulent collective shadow onto the Jewish people. The world had never seen the equal of this mass destruction and carnage.

An entire generation may live a modern, civilized life without ever touching much of its unconscious nature. Then, predictably, it breaks loose in a war or some other form of destruction. We have seen this quite recently in the Balkans and in Rwanda, where former neighbors slaughter each other. Each time this occurs we wonder how such behavior could occur among civilized people. A greater focus on rationality is not the solution, as the history of the twentieth century so sadly proves. The more one-sided we become in our consciousness, the more we are subject to eruptions from the unconscious.

When asked late in his life if civilization would survive, Jung replied that he hoped it would if only enough people would take responsibility for their own consciousness. The repair of our fractured world must begin with individuals who have the insight and courage to reel in their projections.

CHAPTER 6

CONTENTMENT REQUIRES BEING WHO YOU ARE— NO MORE AND NO LESS

Another psychological process that undermines content-ment in modern life is *inflation*. Inflation is a distorted sense of who you are. Modern people have a psychological tendency to inflate like a balloon. The slang expression "he is just full of hot air" captures this experience. When inflated, we think and act as if we are more than we really are; we are filled with high expectations, sometimes even arrogance. Anything that interferes with our willful desire feels like a disappointment.

Modern life pushes us to inflate. Our progress-oriented, "bigger is better," consumer-driven society celebrates "too-muchness." A recent bumper sticker was succinct in expressing this attitude: "The one who ends up with the most toys wins." The West has been busy for decades teach-ing the world how to inflate; in some ways this has become the essence of being American. It is hard to part with something so ingrained as our power stance.

A modern person experiences the treasures of the unconscious, and instantly his or her ego structure snatches them up and tries to run off with them. For example, something good happens, and we try to possess it, or we get arrogant, or we try to exploit it or turn it into a business. The ego thinks, "It's mine! How can I bottle it? How can I sell it? How can I take this home?" We cling to inflations, even mistaking "highs" for contentment, but peak experiences are not contentment. What goes up must come down.

Anytime we puff ourselves up—whether to gain attention, power, status, monetary reward, or love—there is a price. Every inflation is followed by a deflation, and then the hot air balloon comes crashing down. A *deflation*[1] is thinking and acting as if you are less than you really are, a feeling of "not-enoughness." Deflation is displayed through negativity, withdrawal, pulling back, giving up—even shyness. You feel alienated and lonely. At the bottom of a deflation nothing in life is enough or worthwhile.

Inflations and deflations turn life into a wild ride of "too-muchness" followed by "not-enoughness." They undermine our capacity for contentment. Contentment can be found only in the middle place, the point where you are neither inflated nor deflated. It requires that you be who you are, no more and no less.

[1]Jung called this phenomenon *negative inflation,* which we find unnecessarily confusing. We prefer the term *deflation.*

King Lear: Sowing the Seeds of Discontent

In the story of King Lear, some of the characters inflate to dizzying heights, in a style that is very modern, and their attempts to find contentment through wealth, power, and the manipulation of external reality only lead to more suffering. We also see characters deflating to the lowest depths, leading to depression, anger, even attempted suicide. Fortunately, Shakespeare also points the way to a cure for this dilemma.

In the opening scene, Lear has a king-sized inflation. As we have observed, the monarch announces that he will apportion the kingdom out to his daughters. This is an indication of inflation. If you have certain responsibilities, then you cannot suddenly unload those responsibilities. To be anything other than what you actually are is a distortion of reality.

Two of the daughters respond with flowery speeches. Such outpourings of admiration and affection are immediately suspect. Most of us can sense insincere flattery and buttering up; we may hear it from business associates, at a cocktail party, or even from members of our own family. This kind of inflated talk just contributes to an unreality that will create suffering. Phoniness, exaggeration, false sentimentality—these make the king puff up artificially, and they feed his discontent.

However, Lear is impressed with this phony spectacle, which tells us that inflation feeds upon inflation. When our egos get hold of some powerful energy from the unconscious, they may start to identify with that energy. Then we star acting like spoiled kings, demanding that reality be cut to fit our desires.

Jung might well have been thinking of Lear when he wrote, "An inflated consciousness is always egocentric and conscious of nothing but its own existence. It is incapable of learning from the past, incapable of understanding contemporary events, and incapable of drawing right conclusions about the future. It is hypnotized by itself and therefore cannot be argued with. It inevitably dooms itself to calamities that must strike it dead."

In financial markets, experts speak of the "bottom falling out." When this happens, there is always a painful overcorrection. A similar turnabout occurs psychologically. Saturday night's artificial high is followed by Sunday's hangover and Monday's blues. This is the stuff of deflation. It is like having all the air suddenly let out of your balloon.

The Value of Foolish Wisdom

In addition to the scheming and disloyal figures surrounding Lear, Shakespeare's cast of characters includes a fool. There is an old proverb that God wanted to hide wisdom so that not everyone would indiscriminately find it. Accordingly, God decided to place it in innocent children and fools. It is hard to get wisdom out of an innocent child, and we would never think to get it out of a fool. In both cases it is fairly safe.

King Lear calls for his fool and is told that since Cordelia (Lear's youngest daughter) has been banished from the kingdom, "the fool hath much pined away." The fool is a key figure in the story in that he tries to provide protection against

those psychological distortions that undermine contentment. He continually prods the king with the truth, trying to
burst his bubble of unreality. One can learn a great deal from
this. There is a bit of us that simply doesn't buy the nonsense.
The fool deflates pomposity, and he may use humor, foolish
talk, or exaggeration to point out egotistical folly.

We think of a fool as the object of scorn, but if we
would pay more attention to our own inner fool, we could
save ourselves a lot of embarrassment. There is a natural
tendency in the psyche to try to correct for extreme inflations and deflations. Jung wrote that if one is puffed up too
high, it "may lead to attacks of giddiness, or to a tendency to
fall downstairs, to twist one's ankle, to stumble over steps
and chairs and so on." This is the inner fool at work.

The fool is allowed greater latitude than other members of the court. He can get by with practically anything he
wants, because everyone knows that he is, after all, just a
fool. The fool can tumble around without dignity, say disre-
spectful things, even make fun of the king. There is a little
corner for foolish wisdom in everyone's inner life.

The speech of the fool contains some wonderful
advice.

He says, "Have more than thou showest, / Speak less
than thou knowest, / Lend more than thou owest, / Ride
more than thou goest, / Learn more than thou trowest, / Set
less than thou throwest; / Leave thy drink and thy whore, /
And keep in-a-door, / And thou shall have more / Than two
tens to a score."

This is foolish wisdom. The king turns round after this speech is delivered and says, "Dost thou call me fool, boy?"

"You gave away all your other titles; this one you've had since birth," replies the fool. He is so bold as to call the king a fool to his face, and he gets away with it, though the king is slow to learn. He ignores the fool's advice.

It has been said that a fool becomes a sage by letting himself be free to be a fool. A fool can learn many things yet still be a fool, but he becomes a sage when he has the humility to accept himself as he is.

The Role of Suffering

Both Lear and Gloucester suffer terribly in Shakespeare's story. One way of interpreting Gloucester's role in the drama is that he represents a naive acceptance of the consciousness of his time. He is not particularly good or evil. He remains loyal to the king, which has some virtue in it, but he just coasts through an unexamined life without taking responsibility for his actions. When we drift through life half-asleep, we inadvertently hurt others as well as ourselves. Many of us seem to need a deep wounding or loss before we are willing to wake up.

In Shakespeare's story, an emissary is sent by the unholy three (Gloucester's bastard son, Edmund, and Lear's older daughters, Regan and Goneril) to deal with the earl of Gloucester. You will recall that Edmund wants to get rid of his father and thereby seize his power and riches. In a terrifying scene, Gloucester's eyes are gouged out, and after he is blinded this poor man is left sitting out in the cold.

"As flies to wanton boys are we to the gods; they kill us for their sport," Gloucester says. This is the ultimate form of bitterness—to curse the very gods. This is how we may feel at the lowest depths of a deflation.

However, it is precisely at this point of breakdown that a breakthrough is possible. What is needed is not for the ego to give up, but for it to give up its pretensions. The deepest disappointments and sufferings in life bring us face-to-face with the deepest mysteries. Suffering may shake us out of the stupor of a provisional life, shatter our illusions of control, throw over naive and immature attitudes, and force us to consciously consider our relationships with other people and with God.

After this horrible blinding, Gloucester's legitimate son, Edgar, comes to comfort and aid his father. Gloucester is so overcome with pain that he doesn't recognize the voice of his own son, and he makes a terrible request of his companion. "Take me to the edge of the cliffs of Dover," he says, "and then stand back so that I may jump over the cliffs and end my misery."

Edgar agrees to help Gloucester end his life, but he hopes to find some way to cure his father's suicidal urge along the way. After journeying for a while, they arrive at the middle of a cow pasture, and young Edgar is inspired to use a bit of trickery as "shock treatment." Edgar convinces his father that they are teetering on the edge of the steep cliff. He comments on the ships at the bottom of the cliff, noting that they appear so small that you can hardly see them. The fishermen below look like mice, Edgar says convincingly (remember, all of this is really taking place in the middle of a cow pasture).

EDGAR: Give me your hand; you are now within a foot
    Of the extreme verge. For all beneath the moon
    Would I not leap upright.
GLOUCESTER: Let go my hand.
    Here, friend, 's another purse; in it a jewel
    Well worth a poor man's taking. Fairies and gods
    Prosper it with thee! Go thou further off;
    Bid me farewell, and let me hear thee going.
EDGAR: Now fare ye well, good sir.
GLOUCESTER: With all my heart.
EDGAR: Why I do trifle thus with his despair
    Is done to cure it.

At this point in the play, Gloucester throws himself forward, thinking that he is leaping from the heights of the cliffs of Dover, and he swoons. He lands with a terrible thud at the bottom of the cow pasture. Miraculously, the shock of surviving the fall cures him. Through a symbolic sacrifice, he is transformed.

EDGAR: —Alive or dead?
    Ho you, sir! Friend! Hear you, sir? Speak!—

Thus might he pass indeed. Yet he revives.
What are you, sir?
GLOUCESTER [alive and astonished]:
Away and let me die.
EDGAR: Hadst thou been aught but gossamer,
feathers, air,
So many fathom down precipitating,
Thou'dst shivered like an egg; but thou dost
breathe;
Hast heavy substance; bleedest not; speakest; art
sound.
Ten masts at each make not the altitude
Which thou hast perpendicularly fell.
Thy life's a miracle. Speak yet again.
GLOUCESTER: But have I fallen, or no?
EDGAR: From the dread summit of this chalky bourn.
Look up a-height. The shrill-gorged lark so far
Cannot be seen or heard. Do but look up.
GLOUCESTER: Alack, I have no eyes!

Transformation Comes Through a Sacrifice

Having gone through a transformative experience, it is
Gloucester's despair—not his body—that dies. Indeed, for
the first time he perceives that life *is* a miracle when seen
correctly. Enlightenment comes to him in a flash. A short
time later a redeemed Gloucester repents of ever wanting to
take his own life and says, "You ever gentle gods, take my

breath from me. Let not my worser spirit tempt me to die before you please."

Gloucester loses his eyes but gains inner vision. The action of this scene offers a healing balm to anyone who is caught in the despair of a deflation.

Eventually Gloucester does die, though not by his own hand. This in itself is not tragic, as death is the natural goal of life; each of us must eventually die. Shakespeare informs us that Gloucester died "of a heart burst smilingly." After having gained access to inner vision, the earl no longer fears death; it is not a time of worry and despair because he previously died the right way—with a sacrificial act in the middle of a cow pasture. He died to his provisional, ego-centered life and was reborn in the spirit.

Sacrifice is one of the most powerful cures known for an inflation or a deflation. A *sacrifice* involves surrendering your conscious position; it means letting go of getting your way. There are times to push for what you want and times to let go, and it is a wise person who can differentiate between the two.

When you find yourself in an emotional mess or you have painted yourself into some corner or despair has become greater than you can bear or it's three in the morning and you can't sleep (someone once said that the dark night of the soul is always 3 A.M.), you must find a way to sacrifice your conscious viewpoint. Like Gloucester, you must throw yourself over a symbolic cliff of Dover, get up, dust yourself off, and arise with the potential to be a different person.

As shown by the cow pasture, this does not mean literally jumping off a cliff. The tension of modern life can become so great that at times we think the only way out is to die physically, but this is a tragic mistake. Healing and transformation come from a symbolic fall. This is an inner process, and you must not confuse the inner and outer realms.

When someone threatens suicide, it is generally the case that they have misunderstood the process they are facing and are trying to enact a sacrifice at the wrong level. Fortunately, Gloucester had Edgar to help guide him through a difficult time.

We each need an Edgar. In modern courts, this loyal character may be someone on the outside, such as a husband or wife, a companion, a good friend, a counselor, or a therapist. It is highly desirable to have people around who see and accept you as you really are instead of propping up your distortions. In fact, this may be a good definition of a true friend. This loyal character may also be an inside figure, a bit of sanity that holds inside yourself. If this is true, it will see you through the most powerful inflations and deflations that fuel discontent.

Binding the Earthly and Divine Worlds

King Lear is a particularly relevant tale for our time because it shows this cycle of inflations and deflations with high drama. If Shakespeare were alive today and he looked through the window of any home, he would quickly observe all the ingredients of a modern tragedy. The problems depicted in the royal court now pervade Main Street, and it is up to us to create our own masterpiece.

Most people today seem to think that sacrificing means giving something up, such as giving up candy at Lent or denying oneself worldly pleasures. This is how shallow our religious sense has become.

The origins of the word *sacrifice* reveal that its real meaning is to "make sacred or holy." Sacrifice is not giving up something to get something else you want more. Sacrifice is the art of drawing energy from one level and reinvesting it at another level to produce a higher form of consciousness.

Sacrifice is an interior event, but it seems to be greatly aided by external rituals and ceremonies. The ancients would take their best ox, or a goat or a bird, and cut its throat to mark a sacrifice and the acceptance of God's will. We have grown past the need to kill animals, but we have not surpassed the need for meaningful rituals and ceremonies. Many neurotic symptoms are rituals gone wrong.

When done correctly, a sacrifice is never life denying; rather, it is always life affirming. An increasing number of people have lost contact with their cultural heritage or religious tradition, but they can still use tailor-made rituals and ceremonies. To help underscore the transformation of an inner reality, you might blow out a candle, say a prayer, or write a letter and place it under your pillow. You could carve a piece of wood, draw a picture, plant a tree, prepare a special meal, or send a gift to someone in trouble. Some people will fast, meditate, or go to a quiet spot in the mountains or the desert.

The psychological law of rituals is that they should be personally meaningful and should outwardly embody some inner process. This helps us let go of a determined course of action that has collided head-on with outer reality. Properly conceived and performed, rituals and ceremonies bind together the earthly and divine worlds.

Walking the Razor's Edge

When you allow yourself to be taken over by an inflation or a deflation, you set yourself up for a strong dose of its opposite. In Western society we value inflations, even mistaking them for contentment, and unwittingly create our own deflations. A period of thinking you are hot stuff leads to feelings of inferiority and negativity, which in turn whip up our hunger for more inflation. Many people keep this cycle going, until a midlife crisis brings the whole structure crashing down around them.

A little bit of inflation is inevitable, as our moods come and go, but in this culture we tend to push the opposites to dangerous extremes. Alternatively, a healthy life is like walking: you put your weight on your left foot, then the right foot, then the left foot, and so on. There is a natural rhythm of thinking you are a bit more than you really are, then a bit less, then a bit more, and so on. It is necessary to stop every now and then to regain your equilibrium.

Buddhists speak of the middle way and call this balancing act "walking the razor's edge." It is precisely that middle place, where you are neither more nor less than you are, that is the holy place. Most people in the West don't believe that the middle point is the solution; instead we want to inflate, grab hold of emotional "highs" and force reality to go our way. But our appetite for "too-muchness" only brings us "not-enoughness" and keeps us in the painful cycle.

To realize more contentment, it is essential to begin each day by reminding yourself to be just who you are—no more and no less. The inner fool can be enormously helpful in this regard. You might try visualizing a court jester having some fun with you while speaking foolish wisdom about your inflations. A bit of humor often can help put things in perspective. However, when an inflation or a deflation has taken over, the only cure is a sacrifice. This is when you must find your own cliffs of Dover.

CHAPTER 7

CONTENTMENT ISN'T JUST GETTING WHAT YOU WANT—IT'S ALSO WANTING WHAT YOU GET

In China, Taoism instructs that in any circumstance the right action is whatever serves Tao, the greater intelligence working around and through us. In medieval Christianity, the highest achievement was called the Unitive Vision, in which "Thy will becomes my will." India's Hindu tradition teaches that the world is infused with divine energy, and a most holy prayer is *Tat tvam asi,* or "that [Brahman] art thou," meaning that *you* are God. The Bhagavad Gita tells us, "The world is imprisoned in its own activity except when actions are performed as worship of God."

The modern conception of "I" is quite the opposite of what is described in these wisdom traditions. We are taught that each person is a private entity standing apart from all other life in the universe. It seems as if this "I" directs the body like a driver operates a car. It is difficult to locate "I"—

though many would say that it is centered in the brain and leaves off at the edge of the skin.

That captivating rogue and philosopher of the East, Alan Watts, once said that the modern sense of "I" is a tremendous trap. Your body gets tired, becomes sick, and eventually runs down and dies. Meanwhile, Watts noted, we do our best to maximize pleasure and minimize pain in a world "full of stupid people, who are sometimes nice to you, but mostly aren't. They're all out for themselves like you are, and therefore, there's one hell of a conflict going on." He aptly describes the alienation of modern life.[1]

It is natural that we have an identity, this "I" inside; it helps us to grow in many different ways. Most of us have cultural obligations such as earning a living, taking care of our families, and so on, and we need strong and capable egos.

Unfortunately the gift of human consciousness can also feel like a curse. As Watts says, our sense of "I" becomes a lonely and isolating shell. However, there is a way out: the "I" must learn to carry out its daily responsibilities while also serving something greater.

Going Beyond Self-Interest

To gain contentment, modern people need more than strong egos; we also must have access to a source of comfort and wisdom from beyond "I." We experience lack of meaning

---

[1]Alan Watts, *Ego* (Millbrae, CA: Celestial Arts, 1975).

whenever we view ourselves as creatures whose lives have no positive relation to something beyond ourselves. Jung wrote that the decisive question for the modern person is: "Is he [or she] related to something infinite or not? We count for something only because of the essential we embody, and if we do not embody that, life is wasted."

The original meaning of the word *religion* is to rerelate or reconnect—to put back together again, heal the wounds of separation, and to make whole. Contentment grows, not out of pursuing self-interest, but from our capacity to connect to a larger whole—family, social groups, nature, and, ultimately, God. Some people have trouble with the word *God*, but all that is really required here is a willingness to acknowledge a power greater than yourself.

Jung believed that the psychological goal of human life is gradually to recenter the personality from the ego to the Self. Describing this process, he wrote, "Although it is able to preserve its structure, the ego is ousted from its central and dominating position and thus finds itself in the role of a passive observer who lacks the power to assert his will under all circumstances. . . . In this way the will gradually subordinates itself to the stronger factor, namely to the new totality figure I call the Self."[2]

The Self, as Jung defines it, embraces not only the conscious but also the unconscious psyche. The Self is an

[2]Jung, *Collected Works*, 8:224.

"unknowable essence," Jung said, but it might equally be called the "God within us," since all of our highest and ultimate purposes seem to be striving toward it.

To achieve true contentment, our egos must be in meaningful relationship to a steady anchor whose security does not depend upon ever-shifting external events. Depth psychology describes this conscious union as the alignment of the ego and the Self. The process of reclaiming our wholeness requires both the ego and the unconscious, paying due regard to the demands of both.

Whom Does the King Serve?

Shakespeare describes the same process using much more poetic and inspirational language. Recall that at the beginning of Shakespeare's story, Lear rules according to whatever he thinks will bring him pleasure, power, ease, or entertainment. But a king represents more than a single individual; he is the personification of the entire kingdom and must serve a greater whole.

Lear is, in many ways, like the ailing Fisher King from the medieval Grail legend, a man who cannot find a way out of his suffering. Lear's attempt to solve problems using the wrong tools is the central core of Shakespeare's tragedy. His suffering could not have been avoided simply by choosing better. Choosing is the domain of the ego, and it is the instrument of his choosing that must be transformed. He must gain wisdom that comes from a relationship with the mystery that is beyond "I." The King (please remember this refers to your inner King) must serve a greater whole.

We have seen that the earl of Gloucester was redeemed through a sacrifice, as represented by an imaginary leap over the cliffs of Dover. The critical turning point for Lear occurs when he is left shivering out in the rain. The king stops blustering and complaining and instead begins paying attention to someone else. He turns to his companion and asks, "How dost, my boy? Art cold?" As the play progresses, Lear gradually gains humility and connects his suffering with the suffering of other living creatures. He develops his inner capacity for compassion and love.

To Sing like Birds in a Cage

As the story of King Lear draws to a conclusion, the old king is reunited with his one loyal daughter, Cordelia. Both are in exile, the kingdom is in chaos, and the destructive, unconscious forces are competing for power and leaving a trail of wreckage. The armies of Goneril and Regan are about to overtake the camp of Lear and Cordelia. Facing certain capture, Lear makes a wonderful speech.

"Come, let's away to prison," he says. "We two alone will sing like birds in the cage. / When thou dost ask me blessing, I'll kneel down / And ask of thee forgiveness. So we'll live, / And pray, and sing, and tell old tales, and laugh / At gilded butterflies, and hear poor rogues / Talk of court news. And we'll talk with them too, / Who loses and who wins; who's in, who's out; / And take upon us the mystery of things, / As if we were God's spies; and we'll wear out, / In a walled prison, packs and sects of great ones / That ebb and flow by the moon."

This is poetic language saying that he now understands the walled prison of his court and sees with a new clarity and depth of vision the pettiness and intrigues that have fueled his discontent.

This is what each of us must learn to do—to sit in the nonsense of our court with its daily upsets, disappointments, and changes. Court news is all the stuff that fills the morning newspaper: who loses and who wins, who's in and who's out. It all passes like clouds in the sky, and with hardly any more importance.

"We'll live and pray, and sing, and tell old tales, and laugh at gilded butterflies," the king says. That which had worn Lear down and made him so angry and tired before now produces laughter.

Lear comes to understand that the stuff of the court is really about as substantial as the ebbing and flowing of the moon. He accepts the imperfections of the world as part of the play of God. Lear sees it all—the joys and the sorrows, the victories and the defeats—and he can laugh, the merriment of insight, not the derision of bitterness. The enlightened person can participate in the daily frustrations and absurdities of life while simultaneously understanding them as divine play.

Contentment is not found by Lear outside of ordinary experience. He does not withdraw from the world or attempt to escape his suffering. Instead, he finds sacredness in the midst of his anguish.

There is a human tendency to turn even spirituality into an attempt to get what we want. For example, we may pray to God to help us avoid suffering. This represents a fundamental confusion between serving the desires of the ego and serving the divine. We get closer to the divine by accepting that suffering cannot be escaped, but must be embraced as part of life. "Following your bliss" is not a call to narcissism and getting what you want. It is pursuing the rapture that resides at the core of your suffering.

In the tragedy of King Lear we see human suffering pushed to extremes: Lear loses his kingdom, his friend and loyal supporter Gloucester is blinded, he is betrayed by two of his daughters, and his one loyal daughter is hanged shortly after being reconciled with her father. Yet Lear finds contentment!

The example of Lear provides a prototype for how we can work with our own suffering. Neurotic suffering, in which we look for blame and remain victims, goes nowhere. Creative suffering involves affirming all that comes our way—even those circumstances that we don't want and would never choose.

A friend recently referred to a "positive" event in his life as proof that God exists. It was pointed out, perhaps injudiciously, that his faith in God was very thin if he could find the divine only in experiences that he liked. He had a hard time hearing this, but if one clings only to positive inflations for the meaning of life one stands on very insecure ground.

Amazing Grace

Anything that emanates from the personal "I," any decision of what you want or don't want, is one-sided. Contentment requires connecting with a totality that is beyond the apparent contradictions of daily life, a totality that reconciles those contradictions. But you can't just go out and acquire this divine perspective. If you turn spiritual pursuit into a project, going after enlightenment as the ultimate "high," one more "goody" to make you happy, assuage your fears, or remove life's sufferings, you just become inflated.

Many people misconstrue this truth and believe that contentment is the ego getting what it wants. Recentering the personality does not mean manipulating things so that the ego can get its way. You will be greatly disappointed if this is your goal.

Now we are caught in a vicious circle. In seeking contentment, we are like the proverbial donkey chasing a carrot on a stick. If he stands still, he does not get the carrot, but if he chases after it, he still doesn't catch it. What can he do?

The answer is this: you don't need to *do* anything. Your pursuit of contentment assumes that there is something the "I" can do beyond its ordinary tasks, and it is this very conceit that is the problem. It is hard for us to let go of our pride and accept that "what is" *is*.

You cannot acquire contentment like some consumer item, but you can awaken to its gifts. It is closer to the truth to say that contentment comes to us as divine grace.

Discovering Divine Potential

Although you cannot force contentment through an act of will, you can set the stage for its deliverance by seeking out divine potential in ordinary, day-to-day circumstances.

In the Hasidic tradition, great emphasis is placed on finding the divine in daily acts, particularly relationships with other people. The wonderful Jewish philosopher and theologian Martin Buber made a useful distinction between "I and it" versus "I and Thou" relationships. In "I and it" relationships, we treat other people as objects. An object is something that can be controlled, ignored, manipulated, and used for our own selfish purposes. Modern lives are filled with "I and it" relationships.

There is a yearning in each of us to be fully met by others, to be accepted for who we are, and to be imagined by others as the best person we are capable of being. In "I and Thou" relationships, other people are perceived as carriers of shared humanity as well as divine potential. Instead of treating other people as objects to be manipulated, you look for the best possible experience in every circumstance. No encounter lacks hidden significance.

What would your day be like if in every interaction with another you treated that person not just as a means to some end but as the very point and fulfillment of your life? How might it feel if you were treated this way? Such a day would surely bring a real measure of contentment.

Marriage as Spiritual Identity

When we allow ourselves to be truly related to others, our usual boundaries of self luxuriously expand, demonstrating that our sense of "I" need not be a lonely, isolating shell.

The mythologist Joseph Campbell once said that marriage, properly understood, is recognition of a spiritual identity. By marrying or committing to the right person, you create the potential for a greater whole. When there is conflict, each partner must learn to sacrifice their "I" for the unity of the relationship. It is not a matter of "my" needs versus "your" needs, but what is needed by the marriage. For example, if your will is pitted against the will of your partner, ask this: What is needed for the greater good? What will contribute to your goal as a couple or as a family? Of course, this requires that you let go of your "I's" desire to control and get its way. Properly understood, marriage can be a spiritual exercise, the realization of two into a greater one.

Recognizing the divine potential in any situation cannot be reduced to a tidy formula, but one general guideline is to ask yourself what is needed for wholeness in any situation. Instead of asking, "What's in it for me?," you consider, "What is whole-making?" What is required for more wholeness will be different for each person, and it changes constantly. This requires realigning yourself each day, each hour, and each moment.

Grace is in doing. To support its realization you might begin an achievement journal; this is simply a record of how you are attending to divine potential and how your experience changes as a result. When we can live in this fashion, it has a profound effect on the quality of our lives, creating the conditions for grace and contentment.

Getting Past the Oppositions Inside You

Internal opposition can grind our contentment to bits. Most modern people spend a great deal of their life energy supporting this warfare within themselves and opposing their own situation. Just listen to a conversation among friends, and you will hear a recital of all the things that are going wrong in life.

To transform contradiction into contentment requires that you allow both sides of an issue to exist in equal dignity and worth. For example, you should be finishing your work this morning, but you don't feel like it and would rather go for a hike. These two contradictory wishes will cancel each other out if you let them remain in opposition. You might stay in and work with a resentful attitude, or you might take your hike and feel guilty. Or, you could devise a compromise, such as taking a short walk and then settling down to get some work done. A compromise like this can be useful.

An even better approach is to allow your unconscious to contribute to a deeper understanding, putting your life in better perspective and finding a solution that is better than either alternative.

Sit down in a quiet place, take a few deep breaths, quiet the noise of your mind, and listen. The objective is to avoid a neurotic struggle that pits one desire against another. It is valuable to produce good work and to meet your commitments, but it also is valuable to exercise, relax, and play. What is the greater whole that encompasses both these virtues? The exact solution is hard to describe, since it depends upon the particularity of your life and it must arise from the dynamics of the opposing energies that are facing each other.

Perhaps you need to adjust your priorities and your schedule for a better balance of work and play. Maybe you need to become more playful in your work—work and play need not be compartmentalized. Life is creative and explores itself through play. Bring play into your work to discover what is possible.

Listening to the divine voice within is like developing a "sixth sense," which can become more acute with practice. You approach the inner Self with patient expectation, surrendering your own ideas and wishes and humbly asking for guidance. Here is another example: You have reached an impasse in your job and cannot decide how to proceed. Formulate a question in your mind that has a "yes" or "no" answer, such as: "Should I continue with this job?" When you honestly and sincerely surrender to the inner process, an answer will come to you that "feels right." It may be received through a dream, a flood of inner feeling, body language, or in a gesture. It may even come to you in musical form.

When one of us, Jerry, was recently considering a move to a different city he collected all the relevant information, visiting the city, conducting job interviews, and touring potential new homes. This information gathering is the proper work of the ego. Upon returning home, however, he decided to turn the decision over to the unconscious. In a manner similar to petitionary prayer, he asked the divine for guidance. It came spontaneously in the melody of an old song performed by the Beatles titled "Wait." The chorus of that song echoed through his thoughts all day long. The inner guide did not say specifically what to do, but it was abundantly clear that the time was not right for such a move. Although in this example the ego was itching to make a move, it bowed to the wisdom of the Self and "waited."

If you receive nothing in inner guidance it may indicate that you should take no action, that your conscious situation has not yet contributed enough, or that there is a deeper question to be formulated.

Wisdom from the unconscious often suggests an alternative that goes beyond the seeming contradictions of life. It may provide a new perspective or meaning in which the contradiction doesn't entirely go away, but no longer seems important or relevant. To view the elements of life as paradoxical rather than contradictory is to open up a whole new series of possibilities. It is our inability to see a hidden unity that is problematic. To accept paradox is to earn the right to unity. (For an extended discussion of aligning the ego with the Self, please see our earlier book, *Balancing Heaven and Earth*, HarperSanFrancisco, 1998.)

The Daily Dance of Life

The "I" inside each of us thinks that contentment will arrive "just as soon as" it has mastered reality. In truth, contentment is the art of embracing reality. The Upanishads say: This is perfection, and that is perfection. If you mix the two together, that is perfection. And if you withdraw perfection from that, what remains is perfection. This is nice poetry, but what do you do with it? Well, you accept that "what is" *is*. If anything is God, then surely reality must be God.

Unfortunately, it often takes an illness, a loss, or a tragedy of some kind before we realize that individual willpower cannot master reality. When your "I" is ousted from its central and dominating position, it feels like pure suffering. If, instead, you can align your conscious position with something greater, then the suffering can be made meaningful and utilized in life.

Earlier we alluded to Arusakumar, the contented coconut seller in southern India. He sees the will of God in all that crosses his path—the disappointments and defeats as well as the joys and victories. Contentment comes, not only from getting what he wants, but also from wanting what he gets. He accepts that "what is" is divinely inspired.

What many pre-modern people do as a matter of course, because their culture supports them in it, we must achieve as a conscious process. Learning when to assert our wills and when to let go and unconditionally accept "what is"—this is a supreme accomplishment. We can approach this give-and-take as a clumsy, chaotic struggle or as a graceful, choreographed dance. The difference is a measure of our contentment.

CHAPTER 8

WHEN THE WELL OF SUFFERING GOES DRY

In a classic tale from ancient India, *The Ramayana*, there is a sentence that has powerful implications. After the hero, Rama, has undergone tremendous ordeals and successfully rescued his fair damsel, Sita, the divine couple returns to the royal palace to live "happily ever after." But then comes a seemingly terrifying sentence: "But soon the well of suffering went dry, and new discontent had to occur."

The well of suffering went dry!

In other words, Rama and Sita had upset the balance of content and discontent in the universe. How different this notion is from many Western tales in which "they lived happily ever after"!

In *The Ramayana*, to ensure that the world continues to turn, someone starts a rumor that Sita hadn't been "blameless" while being held in captivity by Ravana, an adversary who had abducted her from Rama. King Rama has to punish Sita for a crime that she never committed; he banishes her from the kingdom, and the story goes on to more adventures and new realms of striving, suffering, and reconciliation.

The ramifications of this mythic tale are deeply disturbing. It implies that when we get too contented, some force wells up in the collective unconscious to turn reality in a different direction.

Other spiritual traditions similarly recognize a cyclical pattern. For example, in the liturgical year of the Christian church, Advent is a time of waiting and darkness, sometimes called ember days. This is followed by the light and glory of Christmas. Ash Wednesday ushers in six weeks of darkness, a time to honor the well of suffering with introspection, fasting, and prayer. The "dark" period culminates in Holy Week, when all the statues in the church are wrapped in purple cloth. On Holy Saturday the world is considered to be dead, and even the holy water is removed from the font. Easter Sunday is again the showing forth of the light.

Apparently, when the well of suffering goes dry, something emerges to bring the universe back into dynamic equilibrium. If this is true, then *you must keep your discontent—as well as your contentment—in good shape!* Of course, you don't need to flagellate yourself. Discontent will come to you of its own accord, and when it does, it too must be honored. Trying to control contentment is like wanting Easter without Good Friday. When you start trying to repair or manipulate "what is," then you only upset the natural order of the universe.

As long as you think in terms of this one or that one, you are still caught up in the world of the small, personal "I." But, if you can stand to live in paradox long enough, then a transformation takes place and a new consciousness is born. This occurs when one has stopped trying to maneuver external reality so that it will work out as the "I" desires.

In one Buddhist tradition, when you finally receive enlightenment you have three days to tidy up your affairs because you are about to die. It may be that enduring contentment, in which all the oppositions that fill our daily lives are finally resolved, carries you beyond this world. Without the oppositions that produce discontent, there wouldn't be a dance—life, as we know it, would stop flowing.

In the meantime, we have the wonderful guidance of King Lear, who sees suffering all around him and still learns to affirm life as the play of God. Since we—like Lear—are all in a cage of some sort, we might as well sing, dance, and say "yes" to the whole joyous and painful, miraculous and ordinary content of our lives.

PART 4

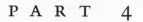

SIMPLE GIFTS
OF
CONTENTMENT

W hat is a gift? It is something that is bestowed upon us, provided without compensation. The best gifts often come as surprises; they are not delivered out of duty or obligation but arise spontaneously. Gifts delight us, but many of us also have trouble accepting them. They may not be exactly what we would have picked out. Perhaps they don't quite fit the image we have of ourselves. And if a gift is truly a gift, we are not in control of the giving process.

In the pages that follow are numerous gifts of contentment, passed along through stories, anecdotes, and exercises. Some require deliberate effort, but many are available just by being more aware of our inner lives. Most of these gifts cost nothing, and they are ever present. To honor and accept simple gifts brings an unexpected measure of contentment.

The Gift of Energy

Contentment requires energy. As modern people, most of us squander our energy as capriciously as we do our money, and as a result, we live at the edge of exhaustion much of the time. We like to spend more than we have. Just as we owe for home mortgages, car payments, and consumer debt, we also push our own energy beyond reasonable human limits.

Bankrupting yourself in energy is just as risky as falling into financial insolvency. When will we make peace with the hound of desire that keeps us on the run?

In a spiritual exercise practiced by many Native Americans called a vision quest, the first requirement is to gather enough energy so that you can stand the vision of the divine when it appears. Similarly, East Indian yoga teaches that 90 percent of the work toward enlightenment is spent preparing your body and mind to withstand an encounter with God. There is an ancient Japanese practice that is said to cure many human ailments: one is locked into a room where there is a toilet but very little else. Food is provided three times a day. It is said that the penitent is tired the first day, sleeps much of the second day, is restless the third day, is climbing the walls the fourth day, is nearly out of his or her mind the fifth day, can hardly remember the sixth day, and comes to a great peace and tranquillity on the seventh day.

Make it a priority to stop your deficit spending and create a savings account of energy. A common phrase for an earlier generation was, "Enough is enough." These days this should be changed to "Enough is already too much."

How can we find this much-needed gift in the midst of busy, modern lives? Honor the sabbath.

The word *sabbath* is of Jewish origin and denotes the seventh one, the end of a cycle and the pause before a new cycle begins afresh. We all need a sabbath, whether we are religious or not. Early in World War II, Great Britain's government was so desperate to produce war goods that the day of rest was temporarily abolished. In response to the war crisis, people were asked to work steadily with no day off. To their astonishment, officials discovered that workers produced less following the new schedule. There were more accidents and many more mistakes with the seven days of work than when the sabbath was honored.

Without the pause of the seventh day (or sabbath), life simply becomes an indistinguishable blur and monotony rules. Your sabbath doesn't have to be on Saturday or Sunday, though this custom honors tradition and fits in with most of our work schedules. The important thing is to schedule a sabbath each week as a time to replenish your energy and refresh your spirit. Don't let duties and responsibilities from the week, even work around the house or social obligations, spill over and claim your energy on this day. Make it a priority to preserve an oasis of rest, contemplation, and spiritual nourishment each week.

The Gift of Fidelity to the Moment

St. Benedict, an Italian monk of the early sixth century and founder of the Benedictine order, had a powerful approach to staying in the present. The word *novice* comes from medieval Latin, and it means to be a beginner, a person who is new to an activity. St. Benedict instructed novices to take a special vow—a vow of fidelity to the moment.

This vow was designed to help support men and women who were embarking on a spiritual journey. St. Benedict's formula is just as relevant and useful as ever. Fidelity to the moment is a deliberate, concentrated attention on what is immediately before you. Focus your full attention on each action, each thought, each feeling, and each sensation. Pay attention to the particularity of the here and now, even in mundane things. For example, if you are washing dishes, notice how the soap swirls over the plate. Let go of the modern tendency to do multiple things at once and instead focus on one thing at a time. Try to view dish washing—or any other routine task—as a worthy activity, an end in itself. Notice how quickly your "I" leaves the present moment and drifts off to replay something in the past or worry about the future. The past is gone, and the future is yet to be. All that exists is now.

To ensure that their focus is never far from the holy now, Benedictine monks return to the church to sing their prayers seven times daily. Similarly, Muslims are called to prayer by the muezzin at special times throughout the day. This is to ensure that one's focus of energy is never far from the contentment of the inner life. Pause throughout your day to notice the fullness of the moment, then carry this fullness back into your worldly activities.

The Gift of Stopping

These days we all need reminders that stopping is possible. Stopping is going nowhere happily, turning away from the hurry that fills so much of modern life. Each day you can give yourself a minivacation by stopping your doing for a few moments. Let go of paying bills, returning phone calls, crossing things off your to-do list, and take some time just to be.

We recently observed an unexpected experience of contentment after arriving at an airport early for a flight and spending a delicious half hour doing nothing. Was it the airport? Was it the collective environment of being in the sweep and flow of humankind? No, that half hour of contentment resulted from having freedom taken away! We could not leave the airport or engage in any of the usual guilt-driven activities that fill so much of daily life. We were forced to simply stop.

One of our favorite quotes from India's sacred scriptures comes from the Katho Upanishad: "By standing still, we overtake those who are running."

One day while swimming at the YMCA, a lifeguard asked one of us, Robert, to contribute a quote for the bulletin board. After some careful thought, the above-noted Indian proverb was placed on the board for all to see. The lifeguard puzzled for a moment over these words and then vehemently said, "No!" She approached the board and wrote the words, "Go, go, go!" Such is the contradiction of modern life.

The next time you are given a few free moments—you get off work a little early, you find yourself alone in the house for an hour, you have thirty extra minutes before you need to go to sleep—try not to immediately fill it.

The Gift of Your Heart's Yearning

Today, all you hear is "I," "I," "I." People are fond of saying, "Where there's a will there's a way," and, "I'll think my way through it." Sometimes, even when we stop doing, the mind just keeps going. Here is a useful exercise for listening to a voice of wisdom that exists outside the "I." In many spiritual traditions, it is the heart, not the head, that is the center of knowing. The voice of the heart is heard in prayer, meditation, and imagination.

Find a quiet place and close your eyes. Place your hand over your heart, and draw several deep breaths. Now think of those things on which you invested energy during the past week. Consider how each of these items contributed to or detracted from your contentment. Now, still holding this list of items in your mind, consider how you feel about this assignment of resources.

As you continue to breathe calmly, shift your attention to your heart, and ask it what is required for its contentment. For what does it yearn? Don't try to answer right away for your heart, just wait and listen. If the answer seems complicated, your outer personality is interfering. For the inner Self things are simple. When you have an answer, compare this with your earlier list. Notice what feelings arise. Then consider investing some of your money, time, and energy in what your heart yearns for as opposed to what your head desires.

To assist your head in surrendering its agendas for a while, here is a story from India.

Once there was a very intelligent man, but unfortunately he was not a very wise man. With his great power he declared war on the gods, saying that he, the intelligent man, could do a better job of creation. The intelligent man lost the battle but was not entirely annihilated. With what was left of his power and intelligence, he went back to the earthly realm and decided to raise up a crop of supermen with which he could challenge the gods again.

The man experimented with creation and decided to grow people on trees, which is much more cost efficient and rapid that begetting people in the old, inefficient way. Trees bore fruit much faster and with less trouble than the human way. All the circuitous paths of courting, lovemaking, gestation, and raising children could be avoided.

This worked out very well, at least in practical terms, and soon the man had a flowering army of supermen who did what they were told. But the gods saw that a terrible error was being committed, and they sent Ganesha, the elephant-headed deity, to add some wisdom to the man's already burdensome intelligence. Ganesha, amazingly, succeeded with this task and convinced the man that he had raised a crop of powerful but unhealthy and useless people.

The experiments had succeeded in growing only the heads of people on the trees, as he thought that this was the only useful part of a human being. The inventor, now more than just intelligent but also tempered by divine wisdom, saw his mistake and repented. He offered to destroy the whole creation of head-only men, but Ganesha saw that a better solution was possible, and this is how coconuts came into being!

The Gift of Nature

In earlier times, and still in a few places in the world, people have listened to the unconscious via oracles, divination, and the voices of nature. Birds, trees, and even stones have been perceived as valuable sources for the whisperings of the divine. Modern people have a bias that only the human head, the ego, and its thoughts have validity, but we too yearn to be touched by something beyond the confines of the personal "I."

The origin of the phrase "to saunter" is good medicine for modern people caught in the too-muchness of life. At a certain point in time, medieval Europeans developed the custom of "sainting" things. We are familiar with venerable individuals raised to sainthood, but the enthusiasm went far past this in the Middle Ages and included inanimate objects. The cross was sainted (Santa Cruz), and even the earth was sainted. This became St. Terre, from which we gained the phrase, "to saunter," that is, to walk on the earth with reverence for its holiness. Perhaps there was an intuition even in those early times that we would need a way of walking with reverence to recall us from hurried lives.

Recently, one of us read a quote from the Middle Ages that set his head spinning: Christ is *constantly* being born in a stable, *constantly* fleeing Herod, *constantly* confusing the elders, *constantly* being betrayed, *constantly* being tried by Pilate, *constantly* being crucified, *constantly* resurrecting. Summoning up this *constantly* into daily life, he took a walk in the desert in search of the fleeting moment that is constant. It was not hard to find. A rock here, an ocotillo in early bloom, a brittle bush plant that had made its brave thrust into life after a recent rain but then perished when no more rain came for several months.

Nature does not ask for explanations, only that we witness the fleeting moment that is constant. Go for a walk in nature and receive the blessings of an ancient tree, listen for a message in the cry of a bird, take counsel with a constant and abiding stream. Allow yourself to reconnect to the creative matrix that supports all of life.

The Gift of Home

It has been said that, in a sense, all sickness is homesickness. Like the extraterrestrial in *E.T.* or Dorothy in *The Wizard of Oz*, we all carry with us a memory and a longing for something left behind. We yearn for home.

What is your image of home? Close your eyes, relax, and allow an image of home to come to your mind. What is the landscape, the season, the time of day? Who is there, what do you see, and what can you smell? Pay attention to the details, and bring your senses into play as you explore your image of home. Now ask yourself, "What is required for me to realize this gift of home?"

Our nostalgia for home shows us not just where we come from, but where we are going; not just our heritage, but also our destiny. Regardless of your childhood experience, home is rightfully a place of belonging, safety, and comfort; it is the place where your most precious treasures are kept.

Here is a story about finding the treasures of home. We are indebted to Martin Buber for his retelling of this ancient tale.[1]

It is told that Eizik, son of Yekel of Cracow, lived for many years in great poverty. Then one day Eizik had a dream. In this dream a voice told him to look for a treasure in Prague. What a mysterious message! Like many of us, Eizik at first ignored his dream, but it came back to him with increasing urgency. Perhaps he dismissed this strange dream as merely the result of indigestion. But when the dream came a third time, it was even more specific: a voice said that Eizik must go to Prague, and there he would find a treasure beyond price under the bridge that leads to the king's palace. Eizik set out for Prague.

When Eizik arrived in the busy city, he soon discovered that the bridge was guarded day and night by the king's soldiers. There was no way he could climb down and begin digging. Eizik wasn't sure what to do. He went to the bridge every morning and kept walking around it until evening. Finally the captain of the guards, who had been watching him, asked in a kindly way whether he was looking for something or waiting for someone.

Eizik poured out his story of the dream that had brought him such a long distance to the bridge leading to the king's palace in Prague.

[1]Martin Buber, *The Way of Man* (Chicago: Wilcox and Follett Co.).

The captain listened patiently, but when he heard Eizik's story he nearly doubled over with laughter. "So to please a dream, poor fellow, you wore out your shoes to come here! How foolish! As for having faith in dreams, if I pursued such folly, I would have had to get going when a dream once told me to go to Cracow and dig for treasure under the stove in the room of a Jew named Eizik, son of Yekel. Yes, that was the name, Eizik, son of Yekel! What a joke! I can just imagine what it wound be like, how I would have had to knock on the door of every house over there, where half of the Jews are named Eizik and the other half Yekel." The captain laughed uproariously and ambled over to the other guards to share the story of this country bumpkin named Eizik.

Eizik bowed politely and immediately began his journey home. Upon arriving back at his own home, he dug up the treasure from the hearth under his stove. He celebrated his good fortune by building a house of prayer.

This story suggests that there is a treasure, the fulfillment of existence, that we search for everywhere. But it can be found in your own home, under the hearth, within the circumstances of your current life. When you find it, you build a house of prayer in your heart.

The Gift of Dreams

We all dream. Short of refusing to remember, we can't refuse our dreams or hide from them. They simply reflect what is. Dreams are an invaluable source of objectivity for a person of integrity. Most of the content of one's dreams consists of elements of the personality that have been relegated to the dungeon of the unconscious. From that place of imprisonment, they make their irrational attempt to find a place in consciousness and assume their rightful role in the personality.

It is safe to assume that every character in your dreams is a "lost" faculty and would broaden your character if it were rightly incorporated into your consciousness. If you dream of Satan or of St. Francis, it may be a shock to think that these are lost aspects of yourself, but this proves to be true if you have the courage to take an objective view of your potential. Both Satan and St. Francis (metaphors for aspects of your character) will serve you well—if you can find the courage to bring them into consciousness and find a useful place for them.

Working with dreams is a complex subject about which entire volumes have been written. (For example, please see Robert A. Johnson's earlier book, *Inner Work*.) However, if you watch your dreams, sincerely try to relate to them, and follow four basic steps, they will give you an accurate illustration of what is happening in your inner life. These steps are:

1.   Write down your dream and make associations to each key image. What meanings can you give the images in your dreams?

2.   Connect dream images to inner dynamics. What emotional or spiritual parts of yourself do the dream images represent?

3.   Interpret. Put together steps 1 and 2 to arrive at the dream's meaning for you.

4.   Ritualize the dream to give it reality. Create a meaningful personal ritual to "dream the dream on" or to bring its potential into the world.

An analyst friend in Zurich used to greet therapy patients at the door of her consulting room with the question, "What did you *do* about the dream we talked about last week?" If the patient mumbled something about having worked on it, she immediately closed the door with the comment, "Come back when you mean business." In her estimation, you had not taken a dream seriously until you had involved the muscles of your body in bringing the dream into the world.

A woman once came into psychotherapy with a wonderful dream. In the dream she was riding in a Boeing 747 at forty-thousand-feet elevation. The plane was full of passengers and running out of fuel, but the pilot refused to bring the jet down. She awoke with a sense of urgency.

This powerful dream was warning the dreamer about an inflation of the first order: she was up forty thousand feet and still the pilot would not bring the plane down! This was discussed with the patient, and she was asked to consider a response that would bring the wisdom of the dream into her daily life.

She returned the next week with a powerful solution. Working with the dream in her imagination, she had the ground crew (that part of the personality that has its feet on the ground, in other words, the ego) disassemble the plane. The woman became conscious of how she had been inflated, acting arrogant at work and alienating her colleagues. She avoided a "crash landing" by sacrificing a bit of her drive for power and slowing down.

Humans are like a highly complex jigsaw puzzle. We need every piece of the pattern to be whole persons. Dreams are a valuable way to connect with the unconscious and correct our projections and inflations.

The Gift of Hidden Purpose

The divine often moves in mysterious ways, and we may only realize its purpose and meaning with the passage of time, as demonstrated by a dark tale from the eighteenth Sura of the Koran. This is the story of Khidr, an angel who directs and helps people. In the Moslem world some people believe that Khidr is responsible for sudden turns of good and bad luck. He serves as a mysterious guide for the Sufis.

One day Khidr comes across the path of Moses, who asks Khidr if he can accompany him and learn the deepest secrets. Khidr protests that this will only lead to trouble since a mortal being like Moses cannot stand the divine perspective, but Moses promises to accept everything that happens, so Khidr reluctantly agrees.

The two wanderers come to a village where Khidr proceeds to drill a hole in all the fishing boats, causing them to sink. Moses starts to complain, but when Khidr reminds him of his promise, he falls silent.

At the next village they meet a beautiful youth whom Khidr unexpectedly kills, and now Moses really protests, but he is reprimanded.

Next Khidr makes the walls of a town fall down. Moses cannot hold his tongue, and Khidr responds that he knew a mere mortal could not comprehend the greater perspective. Khidr insists that the two must part, but before they do he explains to Moses what has taken place. He sank the boats because he knew that a fleet of robbers intended to attack and steal them, and this way at least the boats could be salvaged and repaired. The youth who died was destined to commit a murder and Khidr's act not only prevented the murder, it also saved the young man from losing his soul. Khidr forced the walls of the town to fall because under them was hidden treasure which would now be found by some very poor people who were in desperate need. Moses realizes that he has misunderstood and misinterpreted Khidr's ways, and he falls into silence.

Like *King Lear*, this is a tragic but insightful story. Viewed psychologically, we can understand Khidr as a force in nature that seems to do bad but simultaneously creates good. We need not moralize about why painful things happen or attempt to justify Khidr's actions to see that there often is hidden purpose and meaning in events.

Like the story of Job in the Bible, the example of Khidr reminds us that there is mystery in life that surpasses rational understanding. This is expressed in the everyday expression, "Well, you never know." In truth, we often *don't know* how the slender threads of fate might contribute to the larger tapestry of life. While our conscious "I" must do its best to differentiate and stand up for what seems right and good, it can never know with certainty and there are times when it must wait for the hidden purpose to be revealed.

The Gift of Letting Go

To let go may be seen as a failure, a deviation, from the point of view of the "I." But just as there is a time for seizing hold of life, for taking control and applying your willpower, so there is a time for surrendering to forces that are greater than you. We are indebted to Dr. Mary Watkins for this exercise.[2]

Think of a time when you followed a determined path, doing everything possible from a conscious standpoint to reach a goal, but you still fell short. Recall what that felt like. Now look inside. Who or what in you tells you not to let go? Why does it need to be in control? Spend some time getting to know this inner aspect of yourself.

[2]Dr. Mary Watkins, "Desire" (audiotape), (Carpinteria, CA: Pacifica Graduate Institute, 1995).

Now imagine the situation again, this time letting go of your willful agenda. How might your experience have been different?

Dr. Watkins points out that just as plants wander, sending their roots out in search of rich soil, we too can allow ourselves to move from the known to the unknown. Explore what it must be like to be a plant. Close your eyes and entertain this image in your mind. Drop, for a few moments, all notions of who you are, where you are going, and what you will find. Try to imagine how life might be if you were able to let go of a determined course of action and instead accept what life presents to you. When you bump up against a rock, try moving in a different direction.

Then ask yourself: What situations in my life require more letting go, and how can I achieve this state of mind?

Many people don't like letting go because it seems to imply defeat. But letting go is not the same as giving up. In letting go you consciously do what can be done, but also recognize the limits of the personal "I." Just as there are times for taking the lead, asserting your will, and going after what you want, so too there are times for sacrificing your conscious agenda to what is.

The Gift of Confusion

What? Being confused is a good thing?

To be confused is to be mixed up with and in the swirling midst of "what is." In modern culture, confusion is identified as a mistake or even a madness. In truth, the unconscious reveals itself in moments of disruption. Confusion is an opportunity for your true self to appear.

Instead of rushing to remove confusion, try approaching it as rich with potential. Don't be in such a hurry to chase away these moments through willful action. Try to sit with your confusion, to go more deeply into it with an attitude of expectation. Patiently hold the tension of not-knowing.

This will take some practice. The imperialistic "I" inside of us likes control, clarity, certainty. It wants to divide the world up into "good guys" and "bad guys," but usually life is not so simple. We snub the gift of confusion through impatience. What is needed is for your "I" to accept confusion rather than fear it. Think of this as relaxing a much-overused and overtight muscle.

Become aware of how the urge to act interferes with true knowing. You might even thank those practical, demanding, perfectionistic, and "doing" aspects of yourself for their input, but then redirect your attention back to simply being aware. If you go into your confusion rather than trying to run around or over it, the fear will dissolve and eventually you will gain a deeper understanding of your situation.

Often, the gift of confusion must be honored to clear a space in your life for something new to claim you. To make confusion work for you, reverse the usual procedure: don't just do something, stand there.

The Gift of Paradox

Opposing forces in our lives make us anxious and worried. For example, I want to lose weight, but I also want to enjoy a fine dinner. Which should I choose? I want to go to the party tonight, but I also feel a strong need for rest. Which need should prevail? My budget is overtaxed, but I want a new car. Which of the opposing forces will win? In an ordinary day, we live constantly with warring points of view. The "I" sees the world in terms of contradiction, as this versus that. Contradiction can grind your contentment to bits.

The problem is our inability to see a hidden unity. Reality, by nature, is a paradox. Paradox is the healing balm that we need so badly, for it embraces all reality. Religious experience is typically expressed as paradox, which allows room for grace and mystery.

In paradox, the seeming opposition of two things is seen as complementary. You must allow both sides. Activity has meaning only in relation to rest. It is good to win, and it also is good to lose. Freedom is fine, and so is bowing to authority. Without suffering, we would never know joy. Both sides must equally be accepted and honored.

By accepting both sides of the balance, we change our way of looking at life's problems. To advance from opposition (always a quarrel) to paradox (always holy) is to make a leap of consciousness.

At the ancient temple of Delphi in Greece, a special stone was found with an engraving that said: Measure is

Best. This has been translated as "moderation," but experiencing measure is different from trying to strike a happy medium. Having measure means allowing yourself to experience the pull of opposing forces that are present with any problem. Don't go to half measures; find the measure that can be lived in your particular life on this day.

If you can stay with two apparently conflicting impulses long enough, not jumping into one or the other, you will gain an insight that serves them both. The gift of paradox forces us to move beyond ourselves.

The Gift of Ordinariness

Oddly enough, birthdays and holidays are among the most depressing times of the year for many people. One reason is that we turn them into celebrations of our specialness. Today we need celebrations of ordinariness. The word *ordinary* doesn't mean mediocre, it means ordered. Telling someone they are ordinary is not an insult but a high compliment. To be ordinary means that your life is in order. A friend found deep insight in this fact and ever since has signed his name on correspondence as "Ordinary Joe."

One of us, Robert, once went to a Zen master, hoping to gain wisdom. The custom in this tradition is that you come with a gift and a question. As a gift, he brought a bag full of water plants for the monastery pond. The master accepted this gift with a bow, but when the young man's question came, the master brushed it off with a wave of his hand and proceeded to talk about the propagation of water plants. This conversation went on for an hour, and then the master dismissed his guest.

The next week the seeker again came with a question and a gift: three goldfish for the pond. Again, the master brushed the question aside and said, "Now, as to the propagation of goldfish . . ." He spent the next hour talking about raising fish.

The seeker despaired of such mundane conversation. He wanted answers to life's mysteries. However, just as he got up to leave, the master looked him in the eye and said one word: "ordinariness."

You too can share the gift of ordinariness. On the next holiday or birthday, substitute ordinariness for the desire to be special. This could be as simple as pulling weeds in the garden, straightening your closet, performing a service for someone, or making a basket of paper flowers. Keep your expectations low and your contentment high.

The Gift of Myth

It has been said that science concerns itself with what is true while mythology concerns itself with what is more true. We are always living in some myth, whether we are conscious of it or not. It may be the myth of progress, the myth of the outsider, the myth of perfection, the myth of the hero. Here is a story that reflects the infatuation with technology that is so prevalent these days.

It is the year 2500, and robotics have advanced to a very high level. A young woman is unhappy with her marriage, but she doesn't want to hurt her husband. So she goes to a specialist and has a robot made that is an exact duplicate of her. She has decided to replace herself with the robot, thinking that her husband will never know the difference.

So, she saves up extra grocery money and eventually has enough to pay for the robot. The robot master makes up an exact duplicate, but just as she is leaving with her purchase he says, "Now, there is just one difficulty that you should be aware of. You see, human beings have a heartbeat, and robots have a sixty-cycle hum. I have, however, worked this out by programming the robot to go to your husband and, at first contact, to secretly make a recording of his heartbeat and then duplicate it. This way there should be no problem."

So the woman takes her look-alike robot home and leaves for a night on the town. When the husband comes home, he is greeted by the robot, which, as programmed, records his heartbeat. But all it can detect is a sixty-cycle hum!

This story is not entirely science fiction. A technology expert recently said that a child born today is practically never away from the sixty-cycle hum, day or night. It is characteristic of every fluorescent light, every motor, every electronic device and mechanical gadget. We live at the close of one of the most creative centuries in history, surrounded by miracles of technology. One study estimates that in the average American household, twenty-eight servants would be needed to accomplish the work that is handled by consumer items such as dishwashers, washing machines, and microwave ovens. Such labor-saving devices should contribute to our contentment, but in the process of becoming skilled at controlling external reality, we often lose contact with inner realities.

It is highly instructive to ask yourself: What is the myth by which I live? Did I inherit it from my family, my teachers, my culture? What is the myth that most calls to me? What would that look like in my daily life?

The Gift of Talent

Every person is blessed with special talents. We often think of talent in terms of musical prodigies or athletes gifted with outstanding speed or strength, but talent may reside in any type of activity. Some people are good listeners, others possess the capacity to make beautiful or durable things with their hands, others have an eye for decorating a room. Your talent is whatever makes you excited, fulfilled, and content. The key thing is to find your God-given talent and then put it to work in the world.

If you don't know what your talent is, it may be helpful to review the many different things you have done in life, starting with early experiences as a child. What activities have claimed you? When did you feel passionate about what you were doing? When was there a sense of being taken over? When you are utilizing your talents you feel fulfilled and contented.

Sometimes we abuse a talent. This may take many forms. Generally abuse of a talent occurs when the ego thinks that it is the creator. This is an inflation. As we inflate, the ego becomes dizzy and lightheaded while our work becomes so much hot air.

The great jazz musician John Coltrane spent his twenties running in place, a narcotics habit stifling his musical career. Then, at the age of thirty-three, something happened, and he underwent a spiritual conversion. He renounced drugs and alcohol and created his own quartet. Everyone who worked with him was impressed by his newfound conviction and dedication, both musically and professionally. Coltrane went on to record his masterpiece, *A Love Supreme,* after music became for him a form of worship.

There is an old prejudice that the search for inner knowledge is incompatible with work, yet worship and work belong together. When doing work that utilizes your special talents there is ease and energy. Doors seem to open in unexpected ways. You feel good and have a sense of being at one with your activities and with the universe.

The Gift of Pilgrimage

People look forward to their vacations all year. Vacations are a time when you don't have to do anything, not even answer the telephone.

It is instructive that there is no word for vacation in ancient languages such as Hebrew or Sanskrit. If you were to visit the villages of a premodern culture, you would see people instead going on pilgrimage. There are prescribed pilgrimage places, or holy spots, where there is a general consensus of opinion that something special happened—where a footprint was left by a holy person or a miracle occurred. The destination of the pilgrimage is this special place, and along the way, busy things are curtailed as much as possible. Pilgrimage isn't a painful activity. It is like a country fair in its joyousness. Participants on a pilgrimage have more fun than most Westerners do on vacation.

The essential aspect of a pilgrimage is that you go to a holy site and present yourself to something that is greater than your personal self. This gives value, meaning, direction, and healing, opening the pilgrim to new possibilities.

When Westerners go on vacation, they present themselves to something they think is greater—the ego's pleasure. It is the inflated "I" that must be honored and served. If this is not achieved, then the vacation is a bust. If it rains or the car breaks down or something interferes in some way with their plans, then the whole event is a big disappointment. We take a vacation for amusement and stimulation, and many couples end up quarreling.

Imagine what it would be like if we could view all of life as a pilgrimage or holy endeavor. We would all get up in the morning and dedicate the day as our opus dei, the work for God. All of life—every act—would become sacred and therefore purposeful and meaningful. Even eating would become a communion. Such a perspective brings meaning and holiness into immediate experience.

The Gift of Spontaneity

As modern people, we need to be reminded to move away from the habitual.

Contentment is often found in out-of-the-way places, the shadows, cracks, and crevices of the psyche. Ask yourself, Who is this one inside who likes to take the shortest path, who values efficiency, who needs to feel that something is being accomplished and ruthlessly demands perfection? What is this part of me like? Certainly there is a time for efficiency, but when we become ruled by it, much is lost. Consider what it is like to make a place in your life for the spontaneous, that part of you that takes pleasure in surprise and the unexpected.

In traveling around the world, we have learned that many of the best experiences come from spontaneous wanderings to small, out-of-the-way places, little turns in the road, sleepy villages, intimate shrines that are not on any map.

Spontaneity allows you to be a traveler rather than a tourist. As tourists, we want to know ahead of time what is worth seeing; we become fearful of getting lost. Travelers, however, delight in spontaneity. A chance encounter with a stranger sends you to a remote village or to the hidden monkey forest or to the bungalow rented out by the expatriate's family. The expatriate gets to talking in the bar about life after the war, and—by the way—would you like to see his paintings? He does not show them to most people. For a traveler, doors open that the tourist never sees.

The route of the traveler is often not orderly or efficient. It backtracks, stalls, goes in circles. There is some risk that the traveler may never get to all the "must sees" on the tourist itineraries. But there is a very different quality to the experience of the traveler. It has spontaneity and depth.

At least on occasion we need to risk being inefficient, getting lost, and going "nowhere." Find a new place for lunch, reverse the direction of your walk, take the scenic route whenever you can. Discover those moments when desire and fulfillment arise spontaneously.

The Gift of Forgiveness

For years we have worked with people in analysis, personal therapy, and workshops on the need for forgiveness. This often involves letting go of the memories of parents and traumatic experiences of childhood. We have utilized numerous psychological tools to try to facilitate this, but in the end it seems that most people are not willing to let go until they have something more important to move on to.

The first thing most of us experience is our parents and so they leave an indelible impression upon us, but while you cannot erase that impression, you can grow beyond it. An important step in forgiving your parents is to see them as people. Your healing may be assisted if you are willing to invest some time and energy creating a family tree. Do some research about your grandparents and your great grandparents. What is known about them? What drove them in life? What were their personality traits? What was their relationship to their children? Look for patterns of thought, feeling, and behavior. Then explore the experiences of your parents. How did they meet? What were key events in their partnership? What were challenges that they had to overcome? How did they respond to their own parents?

It is easier to understand and forgive another person when you have walked a mile in their shoes. Many people develop a new relationship with their parents only after they themselves have children. You begin to see that everyone brings skills and limitations to a difficult task, and it is hard work to go beyond the model that you have inherited.

Why is it so important to forgive? Because you cannot hear the inner voice of the divine if you continue to re-injure yourself with old wounds and cling to a limiting sense of self. This applies not only to relationships with parents but equally to all your relationships. An inability to forgive in effect ensures disconnection with God. That is why spiritual traditions of the world all recognize that forgiveness is a necessary step in the path to contentment.

The Gift of Reparation

In twelve-step programs, such as those developed by Alcoholics Anonymous, one of the key steps toward healing is recognizing the wisdom and power of reparation, meaning efforts to repair harm or injury that you may have caused to another. You are instructed to take personal inventory and, where you were wrong, promptly admit it. Then you make a list of all persons you have harmed and, wherever possible, try to make amends. You go to such people and say, "I fear that my past actions may have injured you. Is there something I can do?"

Reparation takes humility one step further by including service to another person. It helps to clear away guilt and shame, which interfere with realizing contentment. Reparation provides a means for cleaning the slate, admitting our limitations, and getting guilt-provoking behavior out in the open. Then we are ready to move on.

The Gift of Compassion

Compassion is empathetic concern for the suffering of another combined with the urge to provide help and support. When we say "I," we are speaking of just one single person, but in compassion there is connection with another living being, and the lonely and isolating prison of "I" that usually separates us is opened. This is why compassion is a gift for both the one who gives and the one who receives.

A basic teaching in Tibetan Buddhism is to practice compassion. It also instructs that our ordinary sense of compassion is often tied up with attachment and centered on selfish motivation. For example, one may feel compassion for one's parents or children simply because they are *my* mother and father, *my* children. But just as the unconscious is not bounded by our skin, so it does not leave off with our biological families. The boundaries of the greater Self extend as far as we can imagine or be in relationship.

Compassion is expressed in any act that reconnects us to the deeper layer of experience that we share with our whole culture and with all creation. Our task is to free ourselves from the prison of separateness by widening our circle of compassion.

Kabir, a fifteenth-century Indian poet, wrote:

Are you looking for me? I am in the next seat. My shoulder is against yours.

You will not find me in stupas, not in Indian shrine rooms, nor in synagogues, nor in cathedrals: not in masses, nor kirtans, not in legs winding around your our neck, nor in eating nothing but vegetables.

When you really look for me, you will see me instantly—you will find me in the tiniest house of time.

Kabir says: Student, tell me, What Is God? He is breath inside the breath.[3]

[3]*The Kabir Book,* versions by Robert Bly (Boston: Beacon Press, 1977).

As Kabir points out, the divine can be found in the particularity of daily life. We simply look for an opportunity each day to tend to the needs of someone in a human way. Small acts of kindness are best for cultivating the gift of compassion.

The Gift of Detachment

Contentment is not a matter of what you possess or don't possess. You can whittle your possessions down to practically nothing and still be miserable. Alternatively, you can be a king in a palace, if that is your job, and realize contentment. Mother Teresa taught that we must be prepared at any moment to give up all our possessions. If we can sustain this *attitude of detachment,* then we don't need to take a vow of poverty. It is your attitude that is key. A story from India is quite instructive on this matter.

There once was a king who, despite his reign over a great empire, was very humble. Each morning he would attend to the political, financial, and social affairs of his kingdom, but early each evening he would retire and sit at the feet of a spiritual master who taught in the forest adjoining the royal palace. The king possessed an elaborate carriage that was carved and gilded and pulled by shining stallions, but when he went to the master he always walked quietly on his own two feet. In fact, the king had let it be known that he was not to be treated in any special way while he was in the presence of the wise one.

Among the group of spiritual seekers who regularly attended the spiritual deepenings, there also was a *sunyasin*. A sunyasin is an ascetic or renunciate in India who owns little more than the yellow robe on his or her back. The sunyasin has renounced possessions, relationships—everything. He or she lives by begging and is completely at the mercy of fate. This man's only possessions were his robe, a begging bowl, and two loincloths.

Day by day the meditation and the teaching went on in the small clearing near the edge of the forest. Both the king and the sunyasin were devoted, and they sat in the front row, one on each side of the master. One day the sunyasin couldn't take it any longer, and he exploded in anger at the master. "Look here," he said. "I have renounced everything to be a holy man. Yet you don't treat me with any more respect than this king who comes here in fine silks, wearing jewelry with priceless gems. He drinks wine and eats whatever he wants from golden plates. He has a harem, servants, and we all know that he partakes of earthly pleasures without end. I have given up all possessions, yet you don't treat me with any more honor than you do this man!"

The master nodded at this outburst but said nothing. Similarly, the king was silent. It is the custom in India that if you ask a question of an enlightened one, you don't always receive a direct answer. The answer may be tucked into a conversation or provided through an example at a later time. This keeps the seeker on his or her toes and helps to distinguish lived experience from mere intellectual understanding.

A few days after the sunyasin's outburst, everyone was again assembled for the master's daily teachings, including the king and the sunyasin. No one had spoken of the earlier conflict. Just as they were beginning their prayers, a messenger came bursting in and, with great urgency, whispered something in the ear of the king. The king nodded calmly, dismissed the young man, and returned to his prayers. A few minutes later another messenger arrived with even more urgency; in fact, he could scarcely control himself. "A fire has broken out, and it threatens the palace," the messenger blurted out before the entire assembled group.

The king nodded calmly and returned to his meditation.

A few minutes later a third messenger came dashing into the clearing and shouted across the heads of everyone, "Your Majesty, Your Majesty, the fire is at the gates of the palace."

Again, the king nodded, but that was all. By this time everyone could see the fire. With great horror, they smelled the acrid smoke that came billowing up from the palace walls. While the prayers continued, the fire raced through the palace, and it wasn't long before it reached the edge of the forest. Ash and smoke filled the air, and soon the members of the devout circle could feel the very heat of the blaze against their faces.

Suddenly, the sunyasin remembered that he had washed his extra loincloth and hung it up to dry in the branches of a tree near the clearing. He jumped to his feet and went dashing across the clearing—but in that very moment the raging fire stopped! The smoke was entirely gone, the sun was again visible, and everyone could see the palace shining serenely just beyond the forest. The puzzled sunyasin stopped in midstride and came back with a sheepish and puzzled look on his face. "What happened?" he asked.

The master replied, "Now tell me, who is attached and who is not?"